HOMICIDE!

JAMES WALTER WALSH: The 54-year-old murder suspect had killed a woman before. The cops called him "the Grinning Hyena." Sasser used every trick in the book to bring him down, but less than two years later he was out—and a suspect in another attack . . .

MICHAEL WAYNE BROWN: He was a stone-cold 18-year-old killer. Sasser put him away for life for the murder of an insurance salesman. The courts sent him to a minimum security prison, and a year after he escaped, he was wanted for murder—again . . .

CRAZY BOBBY: He called himself "Wild Fog" and wrote notes about one of the murdered young women to the cops. When Sasser interviewed him, he said, "I'm Fox from Heaven. I know what happened to Suzanne Oakley. God and I are one . . ."

RICHARD HARRIS: The cops found his wallet in a dead man's car. The married, beer-bellied construction worker didn't look like a homosexual killer, but after a year's investigation and a major slip-up, the cops proved that he was . . .

A former Navy journalist, Green Beret medic, Miami cop and Tulsa homicide detective, Charles W. Sasser is a freelance writer whose articles have appeared in magazines across the country. He is the co-author of *The Walking Dead: A Marine's Story of Vietnam* and *One Shot—One Kill,* both available from Pocket Books.

Books by Charles W. Sasser

Homicide!
One Shot—One Kill
(with Craig Roberts)
The Walking Dead
(with Craig Roberts)

Published by POCKET BOOKS

HOMICIDE!

CHARLES W. SASSER

POCKET BOOKS

New York London Toronto Sydney Tokyo Singapore

Quotes from the *Tulsa Tribune* (Aug. 29, 1975; Sept. 26, 1975; Feb. 5, 1976) have been used by permission of Executive Editor Windsor Ridenour.

An *Original* Publication of POCKET BOOKS

POCKET BOOKS, a division of Simon & Schuster Inc.
1230 Avenue of the Americas, New York, NY 10020

ISBN: 978-1-4767-8450-2

First Pocket Books printing September 1990

10 9 8 7 6 5 4 3 2 1

Cover design by Corsillo/Manzone

Printed in the U.S.A.

This book is dedicated to policemen who have made a difference.

Acknowledgments

I owe many people a debt of gratitude or acknowledgment for either having lived this book with me or encouraged and supported its writing.

During the fourteen years I was a police officer in two cities, I became personal friends with more than six hundred cops, all of whom contributed indelibly to what I was or became as a man and as a police officer. Quite understandably, space dictates that I cannot list all of them.

However, I should like to give special acknowledgment to the detectives who worked with me on Homicide during the critical years covered in this book, among whom are: Sergeant Larry Zane Johnson, Sergeant Roy Hunt, Detectives William F. McCracken, D. A. "Doc" Roberts, Jess McCullough, Jack Powell, Kenneth "Bunny" Brown, Curtis Hanks, Bobby Morrison, George Smith, Fred Parke, Fred Morrow, Harold Harrison, Jim Miller, Tom Nolan, John Hickey, Dave Harrison, and others.

Their stories and their lives are inextricably interwoven into mine.

I should also like to give special acknowledgment

to Chief of Police Jack Purdie, "the Gray Ghost," now deceased, who recognized and put my investigative talents to work; to Dave Highbarger, investigator for the State Medical Examiner's office, who became my friend; and especially to detectives Bill McCracken and "Doc" Roberts, who were my partners and friends.

To my first wife Dianne, thank you for enduring for twelve years. This book will maybe help you understand.

And to my second wife Kathy, thank you for helping me learn to feel again.

Gratitude and love go to my three sons, David, Michael, and Joshua, who were affected in many ways by their father, the cop. I also want to recognize my mother, Mary Louise Wells, who, when I was a kid and we were living in Ozark shacks, built me a desk of old vegetable crates and old boards and helped me believe that I could become a writer.

Author's Note

In this book I have endeavored to render the truth as accurately and vividly as those turbulent years would permit. This is not only my story, but also the story of other people—both policemen and civilians, criminals and victims—who played roles in the events I have narrated.

The dialogues and events reported are to the best of my recollection, and while the content is accurate, I am sure not every quote is entirely accurate word for word or that my interpretation of events will be exactly the same as someone else's. Time has passed since these events occurred.

The names of police officers, my family members, murder victims, convicted homicide suspects, and other law enforcement officials, as well as certain others are the real names of actual persons in this book. However, in some instances names have been changed. As a rule, I have changed the names of witnesses, crime victims other than those who are dead, suspects other than convicted killers, juvenile offenders (those under age 18), and other innocent people somehow involved in these events for whom public exposure would serve no good purpose. Many of these people already have enough trouble in their lives.

CHAPTER ONE

It was a summer's morning, August 28. The sun was hard and red coming up. It turned the Arkansas River into an open artery of blood where it made a wide bend in downtown Tulsa, Oklahoma. A homicide cop would make that parallel. I left the police station and drove, speeding, to the medical examiner's morgue on the westside. You're always in a hurry right after a murder. Statistics prove that if you don't catch a killer during the first forty-eight hours following a homicide, your chances of ever catching him start to decline rapidly. Witnesses disappear or forget, evidence deteriorates, and time crusts over the killer's conscience so he isn't nearly as willing to talk about what he did.

I parked the plain blue Torino in the back alley next to a dipsy Dumpster and entered the morgue through the open back door. The air-conditioning was out again. A thin man with a pallor and a bloody green smock, the medical examiner, was busy at a long stainless-steel tray about to autopsy a small black girl.

The child was naked and lay on her back in the tray, as though only asleep. The tray caught blood and body fluids and drained them off at the bottom. The M.E. revved up a tiny electric saw and deftly made a cut across the dead child's forehead. It didn't wake her. The saw kept going. The room filled with the odor of burnt flesh and bone dust. I also smelled decay. The place always smelled like decay. Sometimes I thought I smelled like decay.

Finishing the circle cut around the skull, the pathologist lifted off the cap, exposing the brain. Glancing up, he reached for a cup of coffee with a bloody hand gloved in rubber. The other hand displayed the skull cap.

"Look at the contusions inside," he directed. "There are also hematomas on the brain. Some of them are old. You can see the scarring. I'd say this kid was beat on the head for months before they finally beat her one time too many. The case belong to you, Columbo?"

Columbo was a popular TV series detective who always got his man, even if he did bumble around spilling mustard on his shirt and looking like he slept in his suit. Austin "Doc" Roberts laid the name on me my first morning in Homicide.

"I think this one's Powell's case," I told the M.E. "My case is Oakley."

"Oh. They brought her in last night."

He looked up from the dissected remains of the black child.

"Suzanne Oakley?" he said.

"Yeah," I said. "Suzanne."

He sipped coffee and made a face at his cup. "Tastes like formaldehyde," he said.

He exchanged the cup for a scalpel, using it to slice across the tiny corpse just below the breasts. Then he cut deep down the centerline from the sternum to the pubis and pried apart the two halves of the body, exposing the intestines. The first time Ken "Bunny"

Brown saw an autopsy, after he came to the Homicide detail, he fainted in his tracks and cracked his head on the tile floor.

"What do you think?" the M.E. asked. "Is there any connection between her killing and the other two girls? What were their names?"

How soon we forget the victims.

"Martin and Rosenbaum," I said.

"Yeah. Geraldine Martin and Mary—"

"Marie. Marie Hope."

". . . *Marie* Rosenbaum. Do you have the same suspect in all three cases?"

"I don't know if there's a connection, and I don't have *any* suspects."

He held up the child's heart dripping in his hands and squinted at it beneath the bright hooded light above the table.

"I heard Jess McCullough transferred out of Homicide," he said in idle conversation. "Does that mean you inherited all three cases now, Sasser?"

I walked over to the open door and looked out against the bright morning. Yeah, I had the cases now. Three headaches.

Sergeant Larry Zane Johnson dumped them on me that morning at squad meeting. He wore his serious sergeant's face. Headlines were already blaring that Tulsa had a Jack the Ripper on the loose.

"We had another girl killing yesterday," he announced, dropping about a ream of reports on my desk. "Put somebody in jail, Columbo."

"You got anybody particular in mind, LZJ, or will just any ol' scumbag do?"

There had been JFK and LBJ, and so we just called Johnson by his initials too. LZJ was in charge of the ten-man day-shift Homicide detail. He wasn't tall and he wasn't fat, but he was a heavy, solid man of about thirty-five with thick hands, short sausage fingers, and an oversized head. He dressed immaculately in expensive suits, but the thing most remarkable about him was his nervousness and the habit that went with the condition. His dark hair stuck to his head like patent leather, but he was always licking the tips of his fingers and running them up to find any stray hairs that might have got loose.

"Suzanne Oakley went jogging in River Park yesterday morning and somebody killed her," LZJ said, licking the tips of his fingers. "She's just like the other two girls. There are no witnesses and damned little evidence. By the way, I'm reassigning Martin and Rosenbaum to you. Jess quit on us. Go out there and find the killer. The chief and the press are on my ass about it."

Now, in the morgue cooler, I flung the sheet off Suzanne Oakley to examine her corpse. The body lay on the gurney in the position it had been found, except faceup now. The arms were still twisted behind her back, the panties and cutoffs down around her ankles, the blue pullover top encircling her neck. Also around her neck were her bra, which had been used to gag her, and a pair of men's black socks that had been tied together and used as a garrote.

Her throat had been cut. There were stab wounds in a cluster in her left breast. A mat of dried leaves and twigs had stuck to the blood on her chest. There was a dead maple leaf, brown but still supple, stuck to her cheek, next to the open, glazed eye.

Yesterday's afternoon-shift detectives had already gone over the body once. I wasn't sure what I hoped to learn by examining it again. I was a "Big Picture" man. I liked to look at a broader scope, but attention to details had paid off for me before. Maybe it would again.

I made notes on the back of an envelope I found crumpled inside my jacket pocket. Everybody ribbed me about my note taking, but I managed. Later, I would transfer the notes to a report.

Dave Highbarger watched as I went over the stiff. He was one of the medical investigators for the M.E. office. He was a lean slab of a man with the most innocent expression I had ever seen on anyone in this line of business. It was like the sordidness around him never touched him.

"Well?" he asked.

That was his way of initiating a little game we had started a few cases ago. He was astounded by the information homicide cops could acquire from just looking at a scene and a victim. I enjoyed the game as much as he did.

"The suspect is right-handed," I began, "of medium height. In fact, not too much taller than the victim."

"Tell me how you know that."

"The angle and depth of the knife wounds and their locations."

"Oh."

"I'd say he's a man in his thirties or later."

Highbarger's eyebrows lifted. I pointed to the black socks knotted around the victim's neck.

"There are no military posts nearby," I explained. "How many younger men do you know who wear plain black military-type socks unless they're in the military? I'd say he's not very clean. Look at the socks. I'll bet they've been worn two or three days. That indicates he probably lives alone."

"A transit?" Highbarger asked. "One of the skid-row habs?"

"I doubt it. The socks are in good shape, only dirty. Our suspect is probably a bachelor or divorced man in his thirties or forties who lives alone in a rented room somewhere on the outskirts of downtown Tulsa. Some freak with a burning anger against broads, a sex hang-up. A mama's boy."

"What possibility do you give on that?"

"I'd go seventy percent."

"And the other thirty percent?"

I shrugged. "Your next-door neighbor. The corner grocer. A schoolteacher. Your preacher."

Highbarger shook his head. He looked impressed. "Can you also look at her and tell me the suspect's name?" he asked.

"I wish I could."

It felt damp and suddenly depressing in the cooler. I started to cover the body again. I paused, looking. "What's this?"

I took out a pencil and poked the eraser end at something clotted inside the dead girl's ear.

"Christ! It's maggots."

CHAPTER TWO

I should have known LZJ would assign me Suzanne Oakley, the jogger in River Park, and that when Jess McCullough transferred to Organized Crime and washed his hands of Geraldine Martin and Marie Rosenbaum, I would be the one to inherit those whodunits too. I had been lucky in solving a few really tough cases, like the Double Bingo Murder and the MFA Insuranceman's homicide. Governor David Boren made the remark, whether true or not, that I was perhaps the best homicide detective in the nation. What that did was ensure that any time a tough case came along, or one the media was interested in—a high-profile murder—it would probably find its way to me for investigation.

"If Columbo can't solve them," I overheard LZJ telling the Gray Ghost, which was what everyone called the police chief, "they can't be solved."

The remark weighed on me. I tugged at the weight of the .357 on my belt. I had watched what that kind of pressure did to Jess McCullough.

McCullough was good, but sometimes you break your balls and come up with nothing. Because of the spectacular nature of the Martin and Rosenbaum slayings, the brass and the news media had been on Jess's ass to solve them.

Now, they would be on mine.

Geraldine Martin, twenty-eight, was the first of the trio to die. A tall and slender coed with dark hair and wonderful blue eyes, she left her art class at the downtown campus of Tulsa Junior College on a cold winter's evening, February 5, to walk to her Volkswagen, parked on a nearby lot. She never made it. She was kidnapped, killed, raped, and her nipples cut off. In that order. Then her nude body was stuffed into a closet in the abandoned Osage Hills Apartments, where it remained for nineteen days while snow fell and the wind whimpered around icy eaves and packs of stray curs prowled, snuffing.

When a construction gang found the body, Jess McCullough happened to be next on the list to receive an investigation assignment. LZJ assigned him the case, but he also threw in the entire Homicide detail for a few days to help question witnesses and suspects and run down leads. As I said before, the first forty-eight hours were the most critical. I didn't envy McCullough this one. Geraldine simply disappeared and her body ended up in the deserted apartments. There was nothing in between. The apartment was vacant, except for a board underneath her butt in the closet, and a little pile of her clothing by her side.

The body was remarkably well-preserved for having been there nineteen days, but then the temperature had been below freezing most of the time. It was like she had been left in cold storage. Just lying there, she was, in the closet with her feet propped up on one end because the closet was too short, with both her nipples cut off neatly, as with a scalpel. Big Bill McCracken, the ex-Marine, couldn't get over that one of the nipples was missing altogether and the other had been stuffed up her vagina. She had been strangled with a cord or something. The thin ligature mark around her neck was deep and cutting.

"I wonder what the pervert did with her other nipple?" McCracken mused.

"Maybe he was hungry," Doc Roberts suggested.

Jack Powell proposed we go around on the streets checking everybody's necklace.

"I knew of this guy one time that killed his girlfriend and cut off her ear to use as a bookmark," Doc said. "We found it in a poetry book. Rod McKuen's *Listen to the Warm.*"

LZJ looked disgusted. "Roberts, go do something. McCullough, I want somebody in jail."

"Good luck, Jess," I said.

Homicide had already started getting to Jess McCullough. He washed his hands a dozen times a day trying to get rid of the smell of death. His lean face grew even more taut and lined as the days and weeks passed. He had nothing to go on—no Big Picture, no details, no witnesses, no evidence. Nothing. A stranger grabbed Geraldine off the streets, did things to her, left the wreckage behind, and moved on. McCullough thought the perpetrator might be a transient serial killer, one of those who moved from place to place like a killing machine, plucking off girls and kids like ripe berries from a vine.

McCullough kept washing his hands and looking harassed.

Marie Hope Rosenbaum came next. Only sixteen years old, and a runaway from the State Training School, she used a false name and lied about her age in order to dance topless at a sleazy bar on The Strip called Satan's. At three A.M. on April 24, three months after Geraldine Martin was killed, another stripper dropped Marie off at a Safeway store near the run-down apartment she shared with her weed-freak boyfriend. Later that morning a motorist on his way to work on Old Sapulpa Road on the other end of the city found *her* nude body thrown across a barbed-wire fence into a field. She had been stabbed sixty-five times. The only thing that held her head on was a little strap of flesh. It looked like the killer had tried to filet out her spine. Her eyes were wide open and staring with unquenched terror into the morning sun. Her clothing, like Martin's, was lying in a pile by her side. Also like Martin, a stranger grabbed her off the street, did atrocious things to her, and left the wreckage behind. There were enough similarities between the two homicides to suggest a common suspect. LZJ assigned the case to McCullough.

The coed and the runaway. The press played them up in headlines, and after a while started questioning the competence of the police investigation. The press always brought up the question of competence if you didn't solve a case overnight. LZJ worried about it every morning at squad meeting.

"The chief's on my ass. Jess, boy, put somebody in jail."

McCullough hunched down at his desk. Doc tried to steer LZJ away from him.

"I got the autopsy back from the M.E. on the Feeney girl," he said.

"Yeah. How'd it say she died?" LZJ asked, switching his attention from McCullough, who just sat at his desk, staring.

"Blowjob," Doc replied, his squirrel eyes bright with mischief.

LZJ stared.

"The report said she died of felony blowjob," Doc said.

Johnson slicked down his hair. "Run that by me again."

"It was an air embolism. Her husband went down

on her and an air bubble got in her bloodstream. She died of acute blowjob."

Powell shook his head. He was tall and handsome in spite of the hardness in his face. He always wore cowboy boots with his western-cut suit and a big silver Fraternal Order of Police belt buckle.

"You should have seen the hole on that bitch," he said. "I don't see how he ever got that balloon to hold air."

LZJ didn't believe it. He kept staring.

"Read the report," Doc said. "How'd you like to live with that—knowing you'd killed your ol' lady with a blowjob?"

Johnson's eyes rolled. But the next morning he was back at McCullough again.

"The Gray Ghost is on my ass."

McCullough finally exploded. "Goddamnit, Johnson! I'm doing the best I can. Reassign the fucking cases if you think anybody else can do better."

LZJ backpedaled if you called his hand. "Jess, calm down, boy. Nobody said you weren't working them."

McCullough looked up. Tears of anger and frustration brightened his eyes. "Johnson, there is no evidence. Do you hear me? *No evidence at all!*"

Solving murders is a job. That's all. You're not supposed to get emotionally involved with them any more than you would get emotional over your die tool if you were a machinist, or your pickup truck. Any involvement is with the puzzle, not with the victim or suspect. It's an intellectual game. You handle it and let the shit roll off your thick cop's skin. It'd kill you if you didn't.

Like Doc said, yesterday's murder went out like yesterday's newspaper. There was always another to take the old one's place. Powell and Bobby Morrison were kicking around a gangland-style snuff-out on East Admiral, Harrison had something going on a junkie-pusher shooting on the northside, Doc complained the fags in tight pants in a queen stabbing were trying to put the make on him, McCracken had a robbery homicide, and I was trying to ferret out a suspect in the killing of a ten-year-old boy who had been abducted and left strangled and naked in a patch of woods south of the city limits. You did your job and handled each one as it came along without getting *involved.* Doc called it job security.

"Our business depends upon people killing each other. Business is good."

But Jess McCullough was letting Geraldine Martin and Marie Rosenbaum get to him.

"There is nothing to go on," he kept saying. "Nothing."

Finally, he had had enough of murders. He transferred to Organized Crime—and on August 27, four months after Rosenbaum and seven months after Martin, it was twenty-four-year-old Suzanne Oakley. All three girls had been killed on Wednesday, if that was significant.

Suzanne got up early to go jogging before she went to work at the Greater Tulsa Metropolitan Planning Commission. Late that afternoon her preacher joined a search party of friends and detectives from Missing Persons to look for her in River Park across from the apartment complex where she lived. The preacher found her body facedown in a patch of poison ivy next to where the Arkansas River curved coming into downtown Tulsa before it shot south along the park for about two miles. She had been strangled, beaten, stabbed, and raped.

Just like the other two women.

"Columbo, the chief is on my ass," LZJ said. "Put somebody in jail."

CHAPTER THREE

There were no female joggers in River Park the morning after Suzanne Oakley was found dead in the poison ivy with her jogging shorts around her ankles. Suzanne's two roommates weren't going to let Jack Powell and me into their apartment. We stood in the August sunshine on their doorstep while they peered suspiciously through the peephole at the badge I held up for them to inspect. They wanted a closer look. I passed it through the crack they opened in the door. They kept the security chain in place.

"Can we call the police station to verify who you are?" they asked.

"I don't blame you."

"The whole city's in a panic over what's happened."

Laura was a thin, washed-out young woman. Jane was shorter and older. She was almost a redhead. They explained that Suzanne Oakley had a routine she followed. Her alarm went off every morning at ten minutes to seven. She brushed her teeth, drew on shorts, a T-shirt, and running shoes, then trotted downstairs and out the back door to cross busy Riverside Drive to the park, where she had been jogging regularly every morning all summer. She had been trying to lose weight.

"It's daylight by then!" Jane cried. "There's always people in the park—other joggers, bicyclists, old people out walking before it gets hot. The traffic rush has started. Didn't *anybody* see what happened?"

LZJ and some of the other dicks were in the park stopping people and asking them if they were out yesterday morning and saw anything. So far, no one had. The jogging path ran within twenty feet of Riverside Drive at the point from which Suzanne had apparently been abducted. Her body was found in a stand of trees and underbrush a half mile south of her apartment complex, fifty feet off Riverside Drive.

I scribbled down on a piece of legal paper what details the roommates could provide about the dead girl and her life. It wasn't much. A few names, some places. A rather ordinary and uneventful American-girl life. She didn't have a regular boyfriend, rarely dated. Her last date had been two weeks before.

"His name's Dewey Kyle," Laura said, bringing coffee in delicate cups embroidered with a blue scroll. "He works in the same office with Suzanne. They went to the movies together. He came and picked her up and brought her home early. Suzanne said it was the worst time she ever had."

"Why? Did he try something?"

"Suzanne said he was a perfect gentleman. He was boring."

The girls tittered self-consciously, forgetting themselves for a moment.

Before Suzanne and her roommates moved to the apartments on South Riverside Drive, they lived dormitory-style at a large house on the southside where they had been studying the bible with a fundamentalist Christian group. The head of the group was an ordained minister and a professor of religion at

Tulsa's Oral Roberts University. All that, I thought, and starting a new religious sect too, must have kept him very busy. His name was Arthur Manis. *Doctor* Arthur Manis.

"Arthur didn't like us to date while we were studying at the house," Laura said. "We had male friends, but if we went coed anywhere, we went in groups. Arthur says that way we wouldn't be tempted to go against God and have sex before we married."

"Who organized the search party that found Suzanne?" I asked Jane and Laura.

"Arthur did," Jane said. "We got worried when Suzanne didn't return from jogging and didn't go to work. When she still hadn't come home by four in the afternoon, Arthur called some of the other men in the movement. They met here and organized to search the park."

"Who assigned the specific areas to be searched?"

"Dr. Manis was kind of in charge. He and Fred found . . . they found Suzanne."

"Do you know how Fred and Arthur came to find the body?"

Laura stifled tears.

"I know what Fred told us," she said. "He said he walked along the riverbank while Arthur went through the middle of the park. You know how narrow the park is. Fred said he suddenly heard Arthur start to scream. Arthur was crying and saying, 'Oh, my God, no!' Like that. Fred ran into the bushes and saw Arthur standing there holding his head and crying. Fred didn't see Suzanne because Dr. Manis wouldn't let him near the body. He told Fred to run for help. That was when Fred ran into that police officer—Dan McSlarrow—who was out searching the park for Suzanne too."

Both girls began weeping. I nodded at Powell and stood up, stuffing my notes into my jacket pocket on top of a bunch of other notes. I wanted to question every man on the search team. Jane tugged timidly at my sleeve.

"Detective Sasser, we've been reading the newspapers about those other girls—Geraldine Martin and the other one from Safeway," she said. "Do you think it's the same man who killed them that . . . that killed our Suzanne?"

I hated to look at the pain in survivors' faces.

"I don't know," I replied truthfully.

"You have to catch her killer!" Laura cried, leaping to her feet and spraying tears. *"You just have to!"*

The August sun was bright and hot outside. I started to sweat.

I guessed Manis to be just short of fifty years old when he showed Powell and me into the office on South Harvard that served as headquarters for his movement. His well-groomed body in an expensive tan suit was short, compact, muscular, obviously in good physical condition. His hair just covered the tops of his ears in a style that made him at once acceptable to both the establishment and to the kids he taught and influenced. My eyes slipped down to where his leg rested over his other knee when he sat down. He had small feet. Size seven. His socks were light blue and matched his tie.

The black socks around Suzanne's neck were about size ten. So was the single Thom McCann–type family-discount shoestore footprint found in the soft soil near the body.

"We believe man's rapid social decline is due to promiscuity in all areas of life," Dr. Manis said when I got him to talking. "Sex is the evil spoken of in the bible. Sex is the serpent that lured Adam into the web of sin. It led to mankind's fall from grace. Therefore, we encourage our young people to date in groups when they date. That way, they aren't placed in a position of having to say yes or no when it comes to sex. It's safer. We should not place young people in a position of temptation."

"Suzanne accepted your philosophy?" I asked him.

"She was a gift from Heaven. She was still teaching part-time for us at the movement when she . . ."

I caught the faltering in his voice before he finished.

". . . before she died."

I leaned toward him. "She didn't just *die,* Reverend. She was raped and murdered."

His eyes darted toward the window. "Yes, of course."

Cops get paid for being bastards.

"Certainly you would know that Suzanne lived with my wife and me for several months when she first came to Tulsa," he said presently, to fill in the silence that I let hang.

I nodded. Suzanne's divorced mother lived in Texas.

Manis looked at me. I waited still.

"I suppose I'm considered a suspect at this point?" he said.

I concealed my surprise in his bringing up that possibility on his own.

"Why should we consider you a suspect?" I asked him.

His window seemed to hold a lot of fascination for him.

"The newspapers made it sound like Suzanne and I were jogging together when it happened. . . ." he said to the window.

"Have you ever gone jogging with Suzanne in the park?"

His eyes snapped back to mine. He knew where I was leading.

"We jogged together when she was living with us.

That was about a year ago. We have never jogged together in River Park."

"How long does it take you to drive from your house to River Park—*if* you wanted to go there?"

He shrugged, still watching me intently, as though afraid I might suddenly lunge for his throat.

"About fifteen minutes, I guess," he replied, "if I get on the expressway at Memorial. Detective, I know what you're asking."

"What am I asking?"

He sighed.

"You're asking if I could have left home yesterday morning ostensibly to go jogging. But instead of jogging, I drove to River Park, killed poor Suzanne for some totally obscene reason I can't even fathom, then returned home before my wife missed me. That is absurd, but I suppose the quicker you eliminate the obvious suspects, the quicker you can get down to finding the real killer. Detective, my car was in my drive until I left for work. You can ask my wife."

I gave him a thin smile.

"I already have," I said.

LZJ thought you couldn't go wrong if you stuck to the obvious.

"Do you remember the Lockwood case?" he asked.

I did, but I knew Johnson would refresh my memory anyhow in order to make his point.

"Lockwood strangled that fifteen-year-old with the size-forty jugs out on East Pine because she *laughed* at him when he was trying to screw her. Remember? It was Lockwood who called the police to say that he had *found* a body in an old shed. He was out in the street directing traffic for us until Dan Allen noticed he was being too helpful and started questioning him."

LZJ licked his fingertips and slicked down his hair.

"Ask yourself, *how* did that preacher find Suzanne

Oakley's body so easily? Columbo, that body was *hid* in there. Just like Lockwood, the preacher *knew* where to look."

McCracken agreed. He suggested Manis was trying to get a little strange stuff on the side.

"Maybe Suzanne laughed at him," he said.

CHAPTER FOUR

Geraldine Martin had been divorced a couple of times. Marie Rosenbaum had been a stripper at a club. The press played up their murders, as it does any sensational sex crime, but that was nothing compared to the headlines Suzanne Oakley began drawing. She rapidly became a cause célèbre, a symbol of the national crime epidemic. It seemed people could be offended more if they thought a victim was a virgin. I couldn't help thinking it was her deflowering as much as her murder that so outraged public conscience.

It wasn't long before parks, a bicycle path, and even a tree were named after her. Some anonymous donor set up a reward fund for the capture of her killer; it grew substantially over the next few weeks. The city responded to a public demand to make parks safer for women by clearing out all the underbrush in River Park, except for the little patch where we found Suzanne's body. I asked that it be left. Businesses all over the city conducted Crimes Against Women seminars, and politicians were quick to get tough on crime.

Every man on the Homicide squad helped work

the case through the preliminary investigation. The Forty-eight Hour Rule. We hauled in and interrogated all the obvious sex-crime suspects—the freak caught masturbating in the apartment complex pool the week before, the neighborhood Peeping Toms, paroled rapists, the loose nuts and bolts of the city. We questioned them, and I looked at the evidence and found it woefully inadequate. A man's footprint in the soil near the body, the tied-together men's socks around the dead girl's neck. That was about it. Nothing else. No real suspects.

Except Dr. Arthur Manis.

The other detectives seemed unanimous in thinking the preacher was my killer. Cops are amateur psychologists. Manis, they said, had a sex hang-up and a guilt complex over something. "Was the preach dipping his wick in her?" Doc Roberts wondered. Guilt and a repressed sex drive, as any cop could tell you, frequently led to an explosion of some kind.

"I'd drag that holy cocksucker in here and jerk his ass off the ground about ten feet until he started squealing in tongues," Sergeant Dave Harrison said. He was in charge of graveyard-shift detectives. "That's your killer, Sasser."

My preliminary verbal jousting with Manis had cautioned me that I would have to give him space and time for his conscience to work on him—*if* he was Suzanne's murderer. So I waited and asked questions and watched, preparing myself for a confrontation with my only suspect. Whisperings circulated around the station house that Columbo was slipping, that I was fucking up a case and letting a killer off the hook. LZJ didn't say anything, but I could feel him watching.

I grew up hating funeral music and hushed voices, but I attended Suzanne's funeral and stood at the back where I blended into the mourners and could observe without being observed.

Tears filled Dr. Arthur Manis's eyes when he took the pulpit behind the wreath-laden casket to deliver Suzanne's eulogy. I taped his sermon. Later, I listened to his taped voice again and again, trying to pick up some slip of the tongue, some nuance of meaning, some reference that betrayed guilty knowledge.

"I come to you on this sorrow-filled day as a friend," he said. "I come as a friend and as a bereaved father in the loss of a daughter. Suzanne's death, I suppose, is all part of the irony of life. Life has stalked us with tragedy. The silent terror struck without giving us time to brace ourselves for it . . . You have the right to know if faith will work when the going is rough. Who needs it if it doesn't work?"

I listened.

"Suzanne is no longer here with us. She is with Jesus our Friend. The Lord gave a friend this word: 'The butterfly has not been crushed, but only released from its cocoon.' Suzanne has gone higher up and knows the secret which we all seek. She has been released from the cocoon, and no one thus released could ever wish to return."

They were all so eager to get to Heaven, but not *now,* Lord.

And I listened.

"Suzanne will not have died in vain if the city streets are made safer by her death, if Christians will unite to pray for man's fate . . . The final word is forgiveness, forgiveness through our Lord Jesus Christ. Keep that faith with Jesus today as we pray over our loved one, our Suzanne Oakley."

I left ahead of the mourners. I blinked in the bright sunlight. *As if prayer made a damned bit of difference,* I scoffed.

* * *

I became so quiet and introspective that my wife, Dianne, noticed it. The boys wanted to go out and ride horses after dinner, but I shrugged them off.

"I've been watching it on TV—about the jogger in the park," Dianne said. "They said that case was assigned to you."

I got up from the table and went outside through the sliding patio doors and sat on the edge of the little back porch. The summer sun was setting. The sky flamed red beyond the wooded rise to the west of the little meadow where the house was. I always told everyone that the sunsets belonged to me. When Dianne and I were first married, she used to say she had never *really* seen a sunset until I came along and showed it to her. That was right after I became a cop in Miami, Florida, before I transferred to Tulsa, back when I was still a kid with big ears and a big grin. Dianne never mentioned the sunsets anymore.

I guess I didn't either.

She came outside and sat next to me. We watched David and Michael playing with the dog Penny. My black quarter-horse stallion Storm had his head across the top rail of the corral and was mumbling in his throat. The chickens were going to roost. It was as far away from the city as I could get it, in the rural wooded hills of a community called Olive. I had chosen the acreage to satisfy a promise I made eight years ago in Miami when I looked at newborn David and promised not to let the street filth from the city touch him.

I made the same promise to Michael when he came along two years later.

Since then I had included Dianne with David and Michael in the category of people who needed to be protected from that other world I lived in. I seldom talked to her about what went on in the streets. It appalled and frightened her. I could still see the expression on her face after the riots in Miami, before I resigned from the police and was going to teach school.

I think, from the way she looked at me after I got patched up at the hospital and an FBI friend of mine delivered me home on crutches, that it was the first time Dianne truly realized what kind of occupation I was in. The ghetto riots had been going on for three days. My white uniform shirt was crusted with blood from when I had carried a wounded kid in my arms away from a project where we cops had killed two snipers in a fight. Dianne just stared at me when I got home. I leaned on my crutches. She gasped at the blood and whiskers and grime and my ripped uniform. Then she let out a little cry and held onto me for a long time, as though afraid if she didn't, I'd be gone again in the thick of it.

"It's awful!" she cried. "We've been watching it all on TV. They said the police started the rioting. Is that true?"

"Goddamn them all," I said.

I had killed a man, shot him through the lungs. His name was Moses. I killed a man named *Moses.* Dianne thought that was why I brooded while I was recuperating.

"Is it the man you shot?" she asked. "Is that what's bothering you?"

"No," I replied. And that was the truth.

It was the times that bothered me. Everything had been turned upside down.

"Nothing makes sense anymore," I said. "They shoot at us and burn buildings and steal everything that isn't bolted into concrete. Hell, yes, there are things wrong in this country. Injustices and corruption and prejudice. There are poor people and everything. But I'm a cop. I'm one of the good guys, *aren't*

I? Then why am I being made to feel that everything is all *my* fault?"

Sometimes I caught Dianne watching me.

"How can you kill a man and it *not* bother you?" she finally demanded. She wore that expression I could not forget, as though she were looking at a violent and heartless stranger.

Did I have to justify things to her too?

"He was shooting at us—at me," I said, trying to be patient. "Had you rather it had been me who got shot?"

"Of course not! It's just that . . . well, it seems no more to you than if you had simply arrested a drunk driver or something."

"I can't let it be more than that," I said.

Tears sparkled in her green eyes.

"I don't want you to be a policeman anymore," she said.

It pleased Dianne when I resigned from the Miami police department.

"We'll all be happier with you teaching school or something else normal," she said.

That was what I was going to do—teach school. Just as soon as I finished college. Me, a tough-talking, rough-around-the-edges ex-cop who'd been in gunfights and patrolled where even the Devil didn't go without an escort—a teacher! But it seemed the thing to do. Several of my cop friends had already been gunned to death. Dianne went into withdrawal at even the thought that one of the dead cops *could* have been me. She started telling friends that now that I was no longer a cop, she didn't have to worry anymore about whether or not I would be coming home from work.

There was something I didn't tell Dianne. I *missed* the action. Being a cop is like having a virus. It stays in your bloodstream until you work it out. Once you have pounded the mean streets, experienced the thrill of a high-speed car chase, battled it out with guns, once you've done *that,* it's a dull road teaching high school.

I dreaded it.

Our second son Michael was born while I was studying history and anthropology at Florida State University. He had short legs, green eyes like Dianne's, and curly dark hair like mine. Both sons had my features. I have distinctive features—ears that stick out, especially with a short haircut, a nose that swoops up on the end and that boxing in the Navy hadn't improved any, a square jaw that could make me look obstinate at times.

Michael was eight months old and David three years old when I received my degree. We loaded up our red VW and headed for Oklahoma where I had been born and reared.

I knew as soon as we reached Tulsa that I wasn't cut out for a teaching routine, of facing each day stuffed into a classroom. I tried, but then I finally went to Dianne. There was snow on the ground, but Dianne's face grew colder than the snow.

"Di, I'm a cop," I argued. "That's what I do."

Dianne had known all along.

"Think of our two sons," she said.

"What will they think of their dad when they find out he ran away because he couldn't handle it?" I countered. "Being a cop is important. Tulsa needs cops. It's a major department of nearly six hundred. I've already checked into it. They want me. That's what I have to do."

"You don't understand, do you, Chuck? You still don't understand."

I looked at her with a blank stare.

"Working on the police department in Miami

changed you," she said. "Everybody who knew you could see it."

"Everybody changes."

"Not like that. I liked the old you better. If you become a cop again, I don't know what'll happen. I don't know what you'll become, but you won't be my Chuck."

"I can handle it. I understand things better now."

She looked away a moment. Then she looked back. I saw that she was afraid.

"I'll be all right," I said. "I *like* being a cop."

She sighed. "If you have to . . ." was all she said.

It seemed to me that being a homicide detective was the pinnacle of any cop's career. I graduated at the top of my class from the police academy and once more took to the streets. "Five months ago," Sergeant Buck Fox wrote in a commendation, "Officer Sasser, unknown to me at the time, was assigned to my squad. In the next three months Officer Sasser made more felony arrests (27) than the entire squad combined . . ." I did a year's hitch with a special twelve-man street-crimes detail, then took the detective exam. My name came out first on a list of nearly two hundred. That and the reputation I had earned assured me of a choice detective assignment. I wanted Homicide, but few rookie detectives went directly to Homicide. That was why it surprised me when Sergeant Larry Zane Johnson looked me up.

"You come recommended, and I've requested you," he said.

When I told Dianne about it, she murmured, "That's nice," and kept on with whatever it was she was doing.

The police department always stood like a wall between Dianne and me. She said it wasn't the police department as much as what it was doing to me. I couldn't see it. I could handle it. It was better when I didn't talk to her about it.

I gazed at the fading sunset and the little meadow where my sons were playing.

"The news said the Martin and Rosenbaum cases were reassigned to you," Dianne said.

I wearily rubbed my face with both hands.

"Everybody on the police department expects me to crack them," I said presently.

"Larry does that to you," Dianne said. "He knows the more pressure he puts on you, the harder you'll work."

I didn't say anything for a while.

"What if I *can't* crack them?" I asked, more of myself than of her. "Jess has been working on Martin for six months and Rosenbaum for three. There was no evidence. There's no evidence in Oakley either. Di, no homicide detective solves *every* case he works. But they expect me to do it."

Dianne kissed me softly on the mouth. We had been married almost nine years, but she still appeared very pretty to me. She sat with me and held my hand while dark thoughts about murder raced through my mind. *If I solve these cases,* I thought, *I am going to have to pay attention to detail and forget the Big Picture.* I thought of Doc Roberts. No one could outminutia him. He once counted and measured fly larvae—maggots—to prove the exact time of a victim's death. I was going to have to do it too. The three dead girls depended on me.

"You could transfer out of Homicide," Dianne said, waiting.

"I can't."

"What you mean is, you *won't.*"

"They depend on me."

"*We* depend on you. The boys and I."

The tough skin a cop drew around himself to keep from being touched by the streets also kept him from being touched by anything. I got up off the porch and walked out to the corral in the dying light. I felt Dianne watching me.

CHAPTER FIVE

Every day LZJ brought in a stack of mail generated by the publicity surrounding the case—notes of condolence, crank letters, anonymous tips. "Fan mail," Johnson quipped.

Apparently, cops weren't the only ones thinking bad thoughts about Dr. Arthur Manis. A few days after the murder, I received a letter from a district judge that contained a single sentence scrawled on a newspaper clipping describing the finding of Suzanne's body.

What if Rev. Manis breaks out with a poison ivy infection in the next few days? the judge commented on the news article that began:

> The body of Suzanne Oakley, 24, was discovered about 6:30 P.M. Wednesday by the Reverend Arthur Manis, who told officers he had often jogged with the victim. Police said she had been beaten with a blunt instrument, stabbed several times, and strangled with her bra. Marks in the sandy river beach indicated she had been dragged to the area and left near a poison ivy vine in the 4500 block of South Riverside Drive.

The man was thinking like a cop. Manis *had* come down with poison ivy. His secretary told me that. It was time to put the heat on him. Make him sweat. Either he killed the girl—or he didn't.

The reverend sounded wary when I telephoned and asked him to come to police headquarters.

"Why? I've told you everything I know."

"We need to go over it one more time, to make sure we haven't overlooked something."

"Do I need an attorney?"

"Do you? Is there something you haven't told me?"

I knew by his hesitation that he didn't want to look guilty by showing up with a lawyer.

"I'll be right down."

"Make him squirm," LZJ counseled. "Put somebody in jail."

I was determined that by sunset I would either have cracked the Oakley case or I would be right back at the beginning with three dead girls and nowhere to go.

It was said around the station that no suspect could stay in an interrogation room with me for an hour and not bare his heart. I had made myself an artist and a scientist in the dirty business of examining men's seedy little souls. I could turn emotion on and off, like an actor, in order to get what I wanted out of people. Good homicide detectives were like that. LZJ once took a suspect to a church and got down on his knees and *prayed* with the man until he copped to killing his wife, his kids, and his dog, and dismembering them. Doc Roberts drove a suspect to the funeral home to view his victim; that one copped too.

One morning the maid at a sleazy eastside motel found a near-naked dead man in one of the rooms with a .38 bullet hole square in the center of his chest. Prosecuting the case depended upon a confession. The suspect was a nineteen-year-old nude dancer and prostitute from off The Strip. Donna was a beauty with long dark hair and big brown eyes. She sat primly in one of the interrogation cubicles with her pretty legs crossed and the hem of her dress deliberately pulled midway up her thigh.

"She's as sweet as sugar on the outside," Detective Ron Trekell said, "but she's a junkie with a lot of police contact. Her heart will cut steel."

Doc Roberts tossed his cowlick out of his eyes and started the questioning while I sat back against the wall and observed Donna's reactions. It wasn't long before I knew how to get to her. You can get to anyone if you know how. The more Doc put pressure on her, insinuating with ugly sneers that she was nothing but a cheap whore rolling a john, accusing her of executing in cold blood a man who refused to part with his money, the more she looked to me for sympathy. I gave it to her, letting her know in subtle ways that I was taken by her beauty.

Anyone who has ever seen a Grade-B cop movie knows the "good guy–bad guy" routine. At the appropriate moment Doc got red in the face, jumped up, thrust his finger in the beauty's face and shouted, "You murdered that man in cold blood and robbed him. That's Murder One, sister, and we have enough to strap your pretty little ass in the electric chair."

He rammed his hands in his pockets, as though to keep them from leaping out on their own and grabbing Donna by the throat.

"You can do what you want, Sasser," he barked. "But I'm through playing games with this little killer."

I scowled disapprovingly at him as he stormed out of the interrogation room and slammed the door. Donna and I were alone. I knew how she felt—isolated and threatened. Vulnerable. I went into my act.

We were two human beings surrounded by a hostile and unfriendly world. I made my eyes mist with tears as I moved my chair close to and in front of her. Slowly, very slowly, drawing out the drama, I reached out and gently thumbed a tear off her cheek. Then I held her chin in my palm.

"Poor baby," I said. My voice cracked, and I struggled a moment to control my emotions. "Poor, poor baby girl. I just can't see someone like you shooting a man without a good reason."

Nothing works better when you're alone and frightened than the touch and sympathy of another person. Donna burst out sobbing. I knew I had the little bitch.

"I'll bet that other detective wishes it had been me that got killed instead of that creep," Donna said with enough venom to kill a healthy man with one bite.

I tenderly brushed a wisp of dark hair away from her forehead.

"Just tell me what happened, baby girl. I'll understand."

The dam burst just like that. The confession she laid out got her twenty-to-life in the joint. Like I say, you can get to anyone if you know how. You use words and emotions like a dipper in a sewer to lift out a person's deepest terrors and expose them to him.

Problem is, using emotion like that gives you a certain contempt for any expression of feelings. Emotion is a weakness.

I couldn't even cry when Dianne's father died; I was very close to him, but I couldn't cry. I just stood and looked at Dianne—and I didn't feel anything. It was like I was empty.

"Sometimes I don't know who you are anymore!" she cried. "I don't know what you think. I don't know what you feel. I don't know *if* you feel."

"It's better to feel nothing," I admitted once to David Freiberger, a rookie I was breaking in to the streets before I went on the street-crimes detail and then into Homicide.

"How can you keep from feeling?" he asked.

"It protects you," I explained. "Start by pretending you don't have feelings like ordinary people. Just function. It's like you're two people. One of you is a cop who comes out and does what is necessary and doesn't let the shit touch him. You wear your cop's skin to keep it off. The other of you, somehow, has to remain a human being."

"That's schizophrenic!"

"It is, isn't it?"

You do things like that because it's necessary. And then you don't think about it afterward.

If the Reverend Arthur Manis was guilty of Suzanne Oakley's murder—and maybe of Geraldine's and Marie's as well—then I had to get to him too.

We sat in the small bare room facing each other on straight-backed chairs.

"God knows I want to help any way I can," Reverend Manis said.

"Leave God out of this, Preacher. God doesn't come into my interview room unless I ask Him."

Our eyes locked. He looked away first, but his back was to the single door. That, psychologically, left him no way to escape. He had already started sweating.

"Reverend, Suzanne must have been about twenty-two when you first met her," I began. "Isn't that a little late for beginning what you call a father-daughter relationship?"

"Suzanne was very close to both my wife and me. I felt as though she were my daughter in God. Maybe that's a little difficult for someone like yourself to understand."

I let it go. We continued verbal fencing for a few more minutes.

"Reverend Manis, sometimes young girls get infatuated with older men. Especially successful and handsome older men they admire. Did Suzanne—"

"Never!"

A little too quickly.

"I didn't finish the question."

"You were about to intimate Suzanne and I were having an affair . . ."

"Was I?"

"I thought I made my position on promiscuity quite clear."

His eyes resembled little animals seeking a place to hide.

"What about Suzanne?" I asked, pressing the attack. "She looked to be a lusty little thing."

"No!"

He was hiding *something.*

"Quite obviously," I continued, "there were times when the two of you were alone together."

"I don't like that insinuation."

"Answer the question, Reverend!" I barked.

After a second he broke and glanced away.

"There were times, of course," he admitted presently. "She lived with us—my wife and me. But it meant nothing. I told you where I was the morning . . . poor Suzanne died. My God, man. I *couldn't* have murdered that girl!"

Manis's wife told me she awoke that morning at seven-thirty, just as the preacher was returning from jogging. That was no alibi.

"Reverend, I'm trying to find out something about her as well as about you," I said more gently. "Did she ever indicate she might have feelings for you other than those of a daughter for a father?"

Evasively: "I'm a happily married man."

"Reverend, could such feelings have developed?"

"My movement is founded on love. *Love.* Detective Sasser, do you know the meaning of the word?"

"I own a dog. *Could* Suzanne have become infatuated with you? I'm certain you would recognize the signs."

I had to break him, make him start talking about it.

He sighed deeply.

"I guess she *could* have, yes," he said.

"Could you likewise have become enamored of her?"

"I didn't!"

Again, too quickly.

"Suzanne was wholesome and pretty and bouncy," I said. I thought of the maggots in her ear at the morgue. "Surely you noticed those things about her?"

"I'm not blind."

"You liked Suzanne?"

"Everybody liked Suzanne."

"You even loved Suzanne?"

"You make *love* sound dirty."

"Did you ever kiss her?"

"Not the way you make it sound."

"Preacher, did you ever kiss her?"

His eyes dropped. "A peck on the cheek now and then."

"Like when you're greeting each other and saying good-bye?"

"Times like that, yes."

"Those pecks on the cheek were innocent expressions of affection?"

"That is absolutely correct."

I had him running. Now to trap him.

"Your wife did not object?" I continued.

"Janet is not the jealous sort. Certainly she had no reason to be jealous of Suzanne."

"You didn't tell your wife about each time you gave Suzanne a peck on the cheek, did you?"

"Don't be absurd."

"Then it's safe to assume there were times you pecked Suzanne on the cheek when you were alone together?"

He hesitated.

"Is that right, Preacher?"

"There were times," he admitted.

"You felt a great deal of affection for her?"

"I've already said I did."

"I suppose you embraced her too?"

He looked suspicious. "I suppose so."

I had studied this man the first time we talked and again at the funeral. He had poise. He was beginning to lose it now. He looked like an imposter in his finely cut suit and his three-dollar-a-pair socks. I couldn't let up on him. If you got a suspect to admit just one thing, usually that opened him up to confess everything.

"Reverend, let's stop playing games. You know what I'm talking about. I can *prove* it, Reverend. There was at least one time when your kiss was more than the peck on the cheek a father might give a daughter."

I was bluffing. For an instant I thought he was going to bat the bluff back at me like a poor serve. But then he faded. He just seemed to fade out. I lowered my voice. It became gently persuasive.

"Don't you think it's time the whole truth came out?" I asked softly.

His eyes hid behind pools of water. I saw the shame in his face, the desperation. I knew I had him. He had been easy.

"Detective Sasser, you must believe me!" he cried. "That one time . . . it was entirely unexpected. I—I don't know what came over me. I—I had such a feeling for that girl. I started to kiss her on the cheek. She wasn't feeling well for some reason, and . . . it was just a little kiss, that's all. A kiss! The flesh was weak and it was sinful."

He stopped to catch his breath. I waited, expecting him to go on to explain tearfully how a sordid affair had led to recriminations and ultimately to the murder of the one he loved. Instead, to my surprise, his gaze met mine solidly for the first time. It was like, suddenly, a rainfall had washed the dust off his conscience.

I blinked.

Was that all there was? A kiss? A harmless little kiss? Had he, like President Jimmy Carter, once lusted in his heart? *That* was his crime?

I had to be sure. Before, I was seducing him with my interrogation. Now, it felt like I was raping him.

"Are you allergic to poison ivy, Preacher?"

He kept looking at me. "Are you trying to say that just because I have poison ivy I might have . . . ? God help us all!"

I leaned toward him. Our faces were only inches apart. I rammed it to him.

"Reverend, I think you killed Suzanne! You wanted to have sex with her, but that godly sense of morality you carry around like baggage wouldn't let you. *She* wanted to, but you wouldn't. That made her a sinner bound for hell, didn't it? So you waited for that cheap little whore on the jogging path Wednesday morning. You keep trying to believe it *wasn't* you in the park, Preacher, but it *was* you. You dragged that screaming sinner back into the bushes . . ."

"Lord, that's not true! Have you gone crazy?"

". . . and you made love to her while the traffic went by less than fifty feet away. She had it coming, didn't she, Preacher? She was a sinner. You know it's true, don't you? I know it's true. Most of all, *your God knows it's true!*"

Manis bolted to his feet. "I don't have to sit here and—"

"You were wearing walking shorts and a T-shirt when you found her body," I snapped. "God help you if you have poison ivy anywhere except on your legs. Drop your pants and underwear and lift your shirt so I can see your belly."

He glared. But then the defiance drained out of his face, along with the blood. He slowly unbuckled his belt. What dignity he retained fell with his trousers to the floor. He stood naked from the waist down. His head was bowed. He was naked to me in more ways than just the obviously physical.

The poison ivy rash stopped at mid-thigh. His belly and scrotum were clear.

"Let's see your arms."

They were clear.

"Turn around."

Clear butt.

I felt something descend on me. I was tired and a little embarrassed for what I had put him through. I hitched at the weight on my own trousers.

"Put your pants back on," I said.

It was over. I turned and started to leave the interrogation room. I heard the rustle of the preacher pulling his pants up. I didn't look at him.

"Preacher," I murmured to myself as much as to him. I felt a weariness coming on. "Preacher, even men of God are all too goddamned human."

CHAPTER SIX

A cub police reporter named Jack Wimer made the link between the three girls public and cursed it with the Jekyll-and-Hyde tag. His piece generated a fresh surge of terror throughout the city when it appeared on the front page of the Tulsa *Tribune.*

I telephoned him.

"Goddamnit, Wimer, you'll have every broad in northeastern Oklahoma afraid to go out after dark. Jekyll and Hyde? That's like telling people Jack the Ripper is alive and walking among them!"

"Isn't he?"

"There's nothing to indicate one man did in the three of them."

"There's nothing to indicate one man *didn't* do them in either, Columbo."

I couldn't argue that.

Wimer was about twenty or twenty-one. His first day on the police beat he showed up at the scene of a suicide in the downtown YMCA. Police were notified when the stench behind the locked door got so strong other residents on the floor couldn't walk by without grabbing their noses and holding their breath. Doc Roberts and I were working it. Wimer showed up among the spectators in the hallway with a handkerchief crumpled over his mouth and nose and a steno pad in his other hand.

He tried to look natural. He had big wet innocent eyes like some rich woman's poodle. Doc winked at me.

When the reporter came up to the door to ask questions, I grabbed him by one arm and Doc grabbed him by the other. We ushered him into the tiny room where the stiff lay on the floor shot through the temple. Doc closed the door and locked it. Wimer stood there trying not to breathe. His eyes watered. They were riveted on the corpse. He got pale. It was our way of initiating new reporters to the police beat. We gave him "the Treatment."

"What's your name, kid?" Doc asked.

Muffled reply.

"What's that?"

"Jack. Jack Wimer."

"Look at this, Jack," Doc said. "Blowback. When the pistol went off, it sucked brains up the barrel. Look at the goddamn worms in the barrel of this gun. Isn't that something? You want to see this, Wimer?"

"No, uh, thank you," came a choked reply from behind the handkerchief.

"Doc," I interjected for Wimer's further education, "remember that old broad who filled a gourd with warm water and was masturbating with it on the sofa when she died of a heart attack? She was dead about three days when we found her. There she lay naked with the gourd in her slit and her slit looking like an envelope full of rice."

Wimer started coughing and gagging.

"That's the nastiest part of a woman," Doc said

mischievously. "Wimer, think about that crawling rice when you go to bed tonight with your ol' lady. Especially if you go down on her."

Wimer didn't get sick. I had to hand him that. Since then, he had taken a special interest in cases Doc and I cracked. He was okay for a reporter.

The headline above his *Tribune* piece blared: JEKYLL-AND-HYDE SLAYER. IF NOT STOPPED, HE WILL KILL AGAIN. Beneath that was a little subheading, a quote from Sherlock Holmes: "Crime is conceived in the imagination and, therefore, must be solved in the imagination."

"Cute, Wimer," I said. "Cute."

> Somewhere in the city, there may lurk a man, tortured by fantasy and driven to act out the most gruesome details of his macabre imagination, who actually murders young women and doesn't know it.
>
> A Jekyll-and-Hyde psychotic murderer loose in the city?
>
> Such is the opinion of Dr. Barry Kinsey, professor of psychology at the University of Tulsa.
>
> Kinsey, who for the sake of theory examined the facts of Tulsa's latest three sex killings in an interview with the Tulsa *Tribune*, has developed a personality sketch of a man capable of such hideous crimes against women.
>
> His most frightening conclusion: the man, if not stopped, will kill again.

"Using a bit of literary license there, aren't you, Jack?" I grumbled.

"Can you say it's wrong—that he won't kill again?" Wimer demanded.

I couldn't argue that either.

The victims:

Geraldine Martin, 28, a Tulsa Junior College student, was abducted after a night class there February 5. Her body was found stuffed into the closet in a northwest housing renovation project 19 days later. She had been raped, strangled, stabbed repeatedly, and sexually molested.

Marie Hope Rosenbaum, 16, a go-go dancer, was taken by friends to an all-night grocery store after work April 27, to pick up a few things before walking the half block to her house. Her body was found April 28 on a county road. She had been raped, strangled, stabbed repeatedly, and sexually molested.

Suzanne Oakley, 24, an early morning jogger, was dragged from the River Park bicycle path August 27 where she was known to jog every morning before work. Her body was found in the thick underbrush by concerned friends at 6:45 P.M. that same day. She had been raped, stabbed, and sexually molested.

"Jack, you'll have every nut and freak in the city calling me and trying to confess."

"Partner, I didn't put in too much detail, did I?" Wimer asked, sounding offended. "I knew you'd need to keep facts secret to sort out the real killer from all the confessors."

I didn't tell Wimer, but the truth was that I had fed reporters some phony facts to make sure the real facts were protected. Only the killer would know which facts were true.

"You learn fast, Jackie-boy," I said.

Each of their case files at the police department exceeds 1,000 pages of notes, interviews, pictures of possible suspects, and a few half-conceived theories.

Fantasy, Kinsey says, is the key to this type of person's actions. (Although not proven, Kinsey's personality sketch is based on the theory that one man could have killed all three women. Although the cases bear similarities, investigators officially have declined to link the murders.)

"Everything he did to the women, he did in his mind before he ever saw them," Kinsey said.

"This type of person will go over everything in his fantasy world before he acts.

"For a while, this fantasy killing will satisfy a need to express hatred for women. But, after this builds up, he is compelled to act," Kinsey said.

"Everyone has fantasies of some sort, but this man replaces normal fantasies with abnormal fantasies. What's worse, of course, is that he acts them out in reality."

The man, who Kinsey characterizes as a loner and an introvert, probably with no criminal record, has a long list of "hang-ups" which he has never been allowed to vent.

"He hates women. He probably has been rejected by women in a dating or marriage situation.

"If he is married, he may well have a very stormy relationship with his wife," he said.

Kinsey recalled other cases similar to this where the man was reared exclusively by women and dominated by them.

"If there were any males in his upbringing, they were probably ineffectual."

Kinsey declined speculation on a detailed physical description, but said the man probably is older than a teenager but not over 45 years old.

Actions against the victims in each case indicated the killer is a man of some strength.

Kinsey said the man probably does not recognize his problem well enough to seek personal psychiatric help. He agreed, however, that the person could be under the care of a psychiatrist at the request of someone else.

Kinsey theorizes the man probably watches many women and will be found in places where women often walk alone.

"This man will watch women and fantasize about having sex with them in various abnormal ways," Kinsey said. "Then he will often seek out a prostitute who will play his game."

Another trademark of the psychotic killer is a quick development of love-hate relationships, Kinsey said.

"In other words, he probably develops fast love affairs and then hates women with little or no provocation."

Returning to the Jekyll-and-Hyde syndrome, Kinsey said the man may be so seriously disturbed that he does not remember anything about the incident.

He may feel guilty, but not know why.

"It is also possible that the man once remembered his actions, but now has blacked them out of his mind completely or rationalized it as the victim's fault."

"Leave the egg domes out of my cases, Wimer. They'd screw up a Betty Crocker cake mix. The killer knows who he is. He knows."

Wimer hooted. "You *do* believe, then, in the single-killer theory?"

"I'm not saying shit right now, Wimer."

Other than his abnormal sex life, he may not exhibit any outer signs of his inner behavior, Kinsey said.

"He may be quite exemplary in other modes of life. The neighbors would be appalled if they found out."

Along these same lines, Kinsey said the man probably is not a pornography fan or involved in other sex crimes, such as obscene telephone calls.

"And although he may rape without killing, the main objective is the murder rather than the rape."

There has been little physical evidence at any of the crime scenes, according to police reports, making investigation difficult.

"This man does not have enough control to stop himself, but he does have enough control to be careful with evidence and his timing. That's why he's so hard to catch," Kinsey said.

Kinsey said the man will probably get caught by *talking about the cases.*

"He won't brag, like an armed robber would, but he will want to discuss the media accounts of the killings. When someone runs into someone in a bar who wants to talk about it and knows more than he should, he may be talking to the killer."

I knew it. The article generated a fresh rash of call-ins. A female voice on the telephone asked, "Are you the detective working them Jekyll-and-Hyde murders?"

"What can I do for you?"

"I won't tell my name, but I read that article in the newspaper and I think my husband is the killer."

"What makes you think that?"

"Well, he's got weird sex habits is why. Do you want me to tell you about it?"

"By all means."

"Just for example, mind you. Last week, see, he brought in this Doberman pinscher and wanted me to fuck it."

I blinked.

"Did you?"

"Well, yeah. Don't you think he's weird?"

I cursed Wimer underneath my breath. The weirdness was just beginning.

CHAPTER SEVEN

You couldn't let the weirdness get to you.

"Columbo, don't ever take any of this shit personal," McCracken advised. "When you come right to the point, what difference does it really make? You're a tough little bastard, but this stuff'll destroy you if you think catching maggots and putting them in jail will ever make any difference. The system is too fucked up."

When I first came to Homicide, LZJ assigned me to McCracken for my breaking-in period. I strode self-consciously into the big detectives' bullpen on the second floor of the police building, trying to appear nonchalant in the cheap baggy suit purchased with my new clothing allowance.

"Welcome to the Cuckoo's Nest," McCracken said in his laconic way as he swung his booted feet off LZJ's desk top. He was a big man with a prominent scar across his upper lip. "We'll have another case soon. It won't be long. People *enjoy* killing each other."

* * *

The Double Bingo Murder was my first big case with McCracken. John Worthington, twenty-seven, had been shot once in the top of the head in the living room of the Willow Creek apartment he shared with Don Anderson, thirty-six, whose body we found in the bedroom. He had been stabbed thirty times or so with an ice pick and then blasted point-blank in the face with a .38. A man shot in the brain often flops around like a chicken with its neck wrung, spraying blood everywhere. Blood and gore painted the bedroom.

It seemed the two men belonged to a pseudo-religious organization called the Ecumenical Movement, a "charitable, nonprofit church" headquartered in Orange, California. Actually, it was just a front to allow the movement to hold Bingo games in "church" on Tuesday and Saturday nights. It dealt in cash in order to hide profits from the IRS. Cash led to temptation. Worthington and Anderson started skimming off more than their fair share from the Bingo receipts. They were living high with eight bank safety-deposit boxes filled with cash. Even a blind Mississippi sheriff could have followed that trail.

When the two Tulsa "reverends" decided to break off from the Ecumenical Movement and start an independent church in order to reap all the profits, they discovered in the worst possible way that their California mentor, the Right Reverend Henry Leroy O'Brien, an ex-convict, tolerated no backsliders. He flew out from California and met the "Reverend" Oscar Smith, who ran the churches in Oklahoma City. The affair ended with the Tulsa entrepreneurs squeezed out of the Ecumenical Movement and then eliminated the old-fashioned gangster way—full of bullets and ice picks.

"It was a contract hit, then?" LZJ said, ecstatic that McCracken and I had been able to piece the case together.

"It was an accident," I corrected. "If this had been a hit, they wouldn't have left such a clear trail."

Johnson looked puzzled. I explained: "O'Brien and Smith didn't go to Willow Creek with murder in their most reverent souls, Larry. They went there to teach the sinners a lesson, and ended up Bingo-ing on both of them."

The way McCracken and I figured it, frail old Oscar Smith from Oklahoma City held Worthington at gunpoint in the living room while O'Brien, who was well over six feet tall, with a stevedore's arms and shoulders, took Anderson into the bedroom to beat him and stab him a little with an ice pick to teach him what poor judgment he used in attempting to break away from the church and start his own religion. Talk about a schism.

Guarded by Smith, Worthington sat on the living room sofa smoking a cigarette. He probably realized he was next in line for Reverend O'Brien's counseling. Only Anderson was a scrapper, and O'Brien had to kill him. When the gunshot went off, Worthington knew his own life was at stake. He charged Smith. Smith shot him twice, once in the body and then the coup de grace in the top of the head.

"Bingo!" LZJ cracked.

Everybody was a comedian.

"Put 'em in jail," LZJ said. "I'll tell the chief you've solved it. I knew you'd be good, Columbo."

If Henry Leroy O'Brien were some poor scumbag who shot and killed his wife and her lover in a Saturday-night spat, he might have drawn tiny headlines at the bottom of page two, and the Public Defender's office would have passed his case on to the next free P.D. in line. But as it was, O'Brien was the kingpin in an interstate multimillion-dollar scam. That automatically gave him status and benefits as a Super Criminal. He arrived in Tulsa on an extradition warrant from California wearing a three-hundred-dollar suit and Gucci shoes and right away pleaded indigence to avoid the IRS. After all, his "churches" were "nonprofit, charitable organizations."

Standing before the arraigning judge in his fine suit and shined, expensive shoes and styled haircut, he said he had no money of his own for his defense. The judge assigned him a *private* attorney paid for by the *state.* None of those young, eager, on-the-job trainees from the Public Defender's office for a Super Criminal.

I hitched up my trousers.

"How come O'Brien doesn't go through the P.D.'s office like every other indigent?" I asked the judge.

"What difference does it make, Sasser?"

"I just remember bringing in a northside dude for shooting and killing another black man over a craps game. He wanted the state to pay for *his* private attorney too. It was a TND, a Typical Nigger Deal, so the state told him the P.D. was good enough for him."

The judge looked at me.

"If O'Brien is convicted," he explained peevishly, "you know he'll appeal it. We have to do everything we can not to give him grounds to win his appeal. Now if that's all, Sasser, I'm busy."

Like Doc Roberts said, "The more money you got, the more justice you get."

O'Brien was convicted of a reduced charge of first-degree manslaughter and sentenced to serve twenty years in the state penitentiary. Of course, he appealed. On the grounds that Prosecutor Jerry Truster inflamed the jury during closing arguments by announcing, "If you believe this [self-defense], then give Mr. O'Brien back his gun." That, said O'Brien's attorney paid by the state, prevented O'Brien from receiving a fair trial. Apparently a fair trial is only considered *fair* if the defendant is found not guilty.

I knew of a murder case in which a young female victim had been so brutally raped, sodomized, and beaten that a judge ruled the murder inflammatory and that it constituted an unfair trial for the jury to know the details of the slaying.

"I request witnesses be refrained from mentioning her name throughout the rest of the trial," the defense attorney proposed.

From then on the victim was referred to only in the abstract as "the deceased." A jury heard the entire case without knowing exactly how the girl died.

Two months before his conviction, O'Brien signed a pauper's oath in order to get his free attorney. After his conviction, he posted a $100,000 appeals bond. During the appeals, which dragged on for over three years, O'Brien remained in California managing his "church" empire—tax-free, charitable, nonprofit. Oklahoma continued paying his lawyer.

The Oklahoma Court of Criminal Appeals ruled in O'Brien's favor. The case went back to district court for retrial. By this time witnesses had disappeared or forgotten their testimony. We heard that old Oscar Smith, who'd testified against O'Brien, had died. That's part of the attraction of a long trial and appeals process. No defendant ever wants a speedy trial. The D.A.'s office had to plea-bargain with O'Brien's attorneys.

For eliminating two upstarts in a bloody double homicide, Henry Leroy O'Brien was eventually sentenced to serve *five* years in prison. The sentence was *suspended.* O'Brien never served a single day behind prison walls for the killings.

"Bingo!"

McCracken merely shrugged. "Lawyers are lower than whale shit," he said. "It's the system," he said. "That's the way it is. You learn to work with it."

"It's all fucked up," I said. "It's a fucking joke."

After that first case, McCracken always tried to keep me honest. "Bingo!" he'd say, and I'd know what he meant. I was getting involved.

"Bingo!" he said to me long after the Forty-eight Hour Rule expired on the Jekyll-and-Hyde case and I was still pounding the streets day and night.

CHAPTER EIGHT

Every cop knows most homicides are committed by someone the victim knows—wife, husband, son, uncle, friend, neighbor, the local grocer or bookie. That's true even in sex killings like Martin, Rosenbaum, and Oakley. There is often a connection between the victim and the perpetrator, however remote. I kept searching for that connection as I probed society's dirty underbelly, running down known freaks, perverts, and paroled sex violators.

One day a young elementary schoolteacher met me at my desk in the detectives' bullpen. She said her name was Janice Lattimore. She blushed often through freckles like those of some pretty third-grader she might have taught. Her hands kept tumbling in her lap. She was so pretty that Jack Powell and some of the other detectives made it a point to walk by my desk and check her out. McCracken ambled over and cleared some of the clutter off my desk so he could perch on one corner. He had his coat off, and the little snub-nosed Colt on his belt looked like a toy against his giant frame.

"He's been watching me," Janice Lattimore said. "I

decided I ought to tell the police about it when I found out he worked in the same office with Suzanne Oakley."

McCracken lifted an interested brow, lit a cigarette and offered the teacher one. She shook her head. She didn't smoke. She perched on the edge of her chair with her knees pressed primly together. She glanced up at me, then back at her restless hands, then up again, waiting for me to encourage her to go on.

I smiled at her.

"What I'm telling you happened about a month before Suzanne Oakley was killed," Janice continued. "I came home one night from a date. I had just finished changing clothes for bed when the phone rang . . ."

"Janice?" inquired a man's voice.

"Yes."

"Janice, I've been watching you change clothes."

Janice cast an anxious look at her bedroom window. The curtains were drawn and the shade pulled.

"Listen very carefully, Janice. Whatever you do, don't hang up the phone. If you do, you'll get hurt just like the other girls you read about in the papers."

"Who are you?"

"Don't hang up the phone. Do what I tell you to do. I want you to take off your nightgown and stand in front of the window so I can see you. I want you to . . ."

A furious blush crept from underneath the schoolteacher's collar.

"It's not going to embarrass us," I said gently.

"Janice, don't hang up. I want you to put your finger in your pussy and then suck your finger. Do it so I can see you or I'll kill you."

Janice slammed down the receiver and turned off all the lights.

"Detective Sasser, I was so frightened. I wasn't thinking about it at first. Then I realized I knew who it was. I hadn't dated him in three or four months, but I know it was him. It was Dewey Kyle."

Dewey Kyle was Suzanne Oakley's last date. Her roommates Jane and Laura mentioned him. I had his name on my list of people to question.

Janice was blushing again.

"There's something else?" I prompted.

"You'll think me horrid!" she cried.

I smiled. "How could I think that about a pretty girl like you?"

A woman will tell a cop things she wouldn't think of telling her mother or her best friend. Janice hesitated, then she blurted it out: "We had sex one time. Only once!"

Everybody was getting into the sexual revolution.

"He was clumsy and fumbled a lot," Janice said bravely in spite of her red face. "He said something really strange. He said he didn't want his mother to find out. Just like that. Then he said he thought he would have been better off if his mother had died when he was born. I mean, don't you think that's *really* strange for a grown man to say?"

It could get stranger than that.

Before taking out Janice Lattimore, Kyle dated a tiny redhead named Gladys Cook who worked in the same downtown office building with Kyle and Suzanne Oakley. Gladys rented an apartment in a huge brownstone overlooking the Arkansas River where it curved out of downtown Tulsa and started its long sweep along River Park.

"I think you've questioned everyone who worked in the building with Suzanne except me," she said, looking impish. "I feel left out. Do they really call you Columbo? 'Just the facts, ma'am, nothing but the facts.'"

I grinned. "That's Jack Webb—'Dragnet.'"

"So it is. Coffee?"

"I don't drink coffee. Tea?"

"Tea it is. You can take off your coat and your gun if you want. It looks heavy."

"I'm fine."

I had tea with her at a little table in an alcove with windows overlooking the river. The sun was going down. It was a red ball. It made the light in the room red.

"How do you stand it?" Gladys asked.

"Stand what?"

"Seeing death and talking about it all the time? No wonder you have such sad eyes. They're sad, but they're very kind too."

I laughed. *"I'm* supposed to do the interrogation."

"Oh. Is *that* how it works? Did you bring your bright light and your rubber hose?"

"Will I need them?"

"Heavens no! I'm a blabbermouth."

I soon had her talking about Dewey Kyle and Suzanne Oakley.

"Suzanne told me her date with Dewey was the worst evening of her life. All he talked about was philosophy and psychology. She refused to date him again, but she was always as bright and chipper as a sparrow. Everytime she saw him in the hallway at work, she'd chime out, 'Hi, Dewey!' Dewey'd just turn around and look the other way. He wouldn't even speak to her. He did the same thing to me when I stopped dating him."

I kept her going.

"I dated him for about two months," she said. "He always acted confused, like he didn't know what to do with his life. He'd pout if things didn't go his way. He even cried once when we went out for dinner and he accidentally spilled a drink in his lap. He's thirty years old, but I started feeling more like his mother than his date. He wouldn't even kiss me unless he asked me first. I finally broke up with him.

"Dewey went kind of weird. Odd. Like, one night I came home and opened the refrigerator and found a half-empty bottle of wine Dewey had bought on our last dinner date. I changed the lock on my door and stopped hiding the key under the mat. I can't say exactly why, but I was afraid of him.

"One night about midnight he called me on the telephone. He was crying and going on. He said he was going to commit suicide, but a friend talked him out of it. He was irrational. He kept begging me to tell him what was wrong with him. He said he couldn't do anything right. He said everything he touched turned to shit. He said everybody would be better off if he died and just got out of the way. He kept talking like that for an hour. Then he said something crazy, like maybe he should kill his mother instead."

Gladys sipped her tea. Her eyes lifted to watch me from across the table. She looked worried.

"I really started getting frightened. My doorbell would ring late at night, but no one was ever there. Once, I looked out the window and saw Dewey getting in his car and leaving. I accused him of it at work, but he denied it. The doorbell hasn't rung anymore, though. After that he would glare at me like he hated me."

Parts of the Jekyll-and-Hyde profile Jack Wimer wrote about flashed through my mind: "express hatred for women . . . long list of hang-ups . . . rejected by women in a dating or marriage situation . . . reared by women and dominated by them . . . develops fast love affairs and then hates women with little or no provocation."

The profile seemed tailor-made for what I was learning about Dewey Kyle.

Gladys broke through my reveries.

"Huh?"

"Do you think Dewey might really have killed Suzanne?"

His most frightening conclusion: the man, if not stopped, will kill again.

"Good tea," I said, toasting Gladys with the cup.

McCracken asked me the same question. Did Kyle do it?

"Maybe he killed the others too," he said. McCracken was always quick to jump to a conclusion. Give him the slightest reason and he'd jump to a conclusion like a duck on a june bug.

"What about the preacher?" I asked. "I thought you said he did it."

"Put somebody in jail, Columbo," LZJ said.

There was only one flaw in the Dewey Kyle Jekyll-and-Hyde profile: "the man probably does not recognize his problem well enough to seek personal psychiatric help." Not so. Kyle attended group therapy Thursday nights at the Tulsa Psychiatric Foundation. I picked up rumors about a bizarre session that occurred the night after we found the dead jogger. It took some wheedling, and a conversation with a judge about how far the law on privileged communications extended, before Kyle's counselor would talk to me. Concern etched her forehead.

"I wanted to tell someone about it all along," she said, then described how Dewey Kyle stood up before the group that Thursday night and broke out sobbing. He said he had to talk.

"I might be the cause of her dying," he announced.

A hush fell like a shroud over the room. Everyone glanced apprehensively at everyone else.

"Suzanne Oakley was beaten, stabbed, and raped yesterday," Kyle went on, still sobbing. "I feel like I'm

personally involved. I'm in agony right now. I went through this last year. I can identify with whoever killed Suzanne because I've also had crazy, violent fantasies about women. I can even imagine how the killing was done."

No one stirred. You could hear the others breathing.

"I woke up this morning wondering, 'Could I have gone crazy and done it?' I was so angry last year with Gladys Cook that I started carrying a razor, and I felt a strong compulsion to use it on her. I understand how the killer might feel, but my head tells me I just couldn't have done a thing like that."

There was one other thing Jack Wimer included in his Jekyll-and-Hyde profile: "Kinsey said the man will probably get caught by talking about the case."

CHAPTER NINE

I let Dewey Kyle sit in the interrogation cubicle for a while by himself with the door closed while I stood just outside in the detectives' bullpen and took a deep breath. LZJ got up from his desk in Homicide's corner of the room. For one of the first times in his life he had absolutely nothing to say. He just walked over, slapped me on the shoulder, and walked on by. He knew how hard it was. I had seen him come out of an interrogation dripping with perspiration. An interrogation made *you* sweat more than it did the killer.

I took another deep breath and went into the cubicle where a thousand murderers had dropped their guilts and Reverend Arthur Manis had dropped his pants. I stared disbelievingly at the man who, from all indications, might well be Suzanne Oakley's killer —and perhaps Geraldine Martin's and Marie Rosenbaum's as well. He was so damned meek-looking. He was tall and soft-looking, with a roll of baby fat around his middle and thick lenses snugged against a baby's face so pale it appeared never to have seen sunlight. He looked back with a "pardon me for living" expression.

I sat down and got him to talking, disposing of the preliminaries and warming him up. He gave his address as a rented apartment in the 1700 block of South Denver Avenue, one block from Riverside Drive at the upper end of River Park and a little over a mile from Suzanne's apartment. Faltering and stuttering, he ran down his activities on the morning of Suzanne's slaying.

He said he awoke at seven A.M., took a shower, hard-boiled two eggs, watched the morning news on TV, stopped for gas on his way to work, and arrived in his office at eight-ten A.M. Suzanne Oakley died sometime between when Kyle supposedly took a shower and stopped for gas.

"When did you find out Suzanne was missing?" I asked him.

We were getting down to business.

"It must have been after eleven," he replied hesitantly. "Jane was telling everyone at work that Suzanne had gone jogging and hadn't returned."

"What was your reaction?"

"I was concerned, of course."

"I understand you were very upset."

"I was afraid she might have been jogging and fallen into one of those construction ditches where they're working in the park. It gave me an eerie feeling."

Interrogation is a mental game that calls for repeating and reexamining key points of a story, testing to see where the subject stumbles. Mild-looking Dewey Kyle batted his calf eyes behind thick lenses and doggedly continued in a puzzled and distracted manner, as though he had some kind of struggle going on inside that was much more demanding than the real one in which we were engaged.

"Mr. Sasser, *look* at me. Do you really think I'm capable of something like *that?*"

"What do *you* think, Dewey?"

Alarm wrote itself all over the tortured mask of his face.

"I don't know either!" he cried. "God help me. I don't *know* if I did it!"

Christ! This was no act he was putting on.

"Let's work on it together, then," I proposed. "We have to find out. Maybe you're blocking it out subconsciously."

I pursued him into the strange, dark recesses of his mind.

"Dewey, did it make you angry when Suzanne refused to go out with you again after that first time?"

"I didn't ask her to go out with me again. I got busy and—"

I couldn't let him hide from it.

"Dewey! You asked her and she refused. Let's face up to the truths we do know."

"I—" His chin falling on his chest dislodged his glasses. He absently propped them back on his nose. "She refused me," he admitted.

"Gladys broke up with you. So did Janice Lattimore. Now Suzanne rejected you. Were you angry?"

"No."

"Dewey, you wouldn't even speak to Suzanne the entire week before she was killed."

He looked at me and shook his head. "I guess I *was* angry."

"Is it possible you transferred your anger against Gladys and Janice to Suzanne—and *that* was why you hurt Suzanne?"

"No! No! No!"

"Think about it, Dewey!" I snapped. *"Could* it have happened?"

"I don't know."

He screamed it. His glasses misted over. He clawed at his face with both hands. He was trapped. I couldn't let the miserable bastard get away from me.

He looked up at me. His eyes were glazed.

"Maybe it did happen," he said.

"Tell me about it. Can you remember?"

He got very quiet and still. He looked inside himself again, searching.

"I feel guilty like it happened," he whispered. "Am I capable of something like that? I don't know. I really thought about killing Gladys. She hurt me when she broke off. I wouldn't go through with it, but I thought about it. I was very angry."

He started drifting off.

"Dewey?"

"Mr. Sasser, I just sometimes feel guilty about things. One time I read in *Time* magazine about this guy in Florida who killed a girl and dumped her body in a swamp. I read about it and I started feeling guilty. They'd already caught the guy and convicted him, but I wrote a letter to the police in Florida telling them I thought I had killed her instead of the guy they had in jail. See what I mean?"

Christ!

I leaned toward him. "We have to go on, Dewey," I said.

I had to find out.

He still looked introspective. He was drifting.

"Dewey?"

Something gripped his soft frame and shook it.

"I sometimes see it," he said, whispering, his eyes magnified and frightened behind his glasses. "I see it like I'm daydreaming or something."

I remembered Jack Lazar. Evidence pointed to the fact that Lazar stalked a telephone operator after she got off work. He stalked her into a snowstorm, caught her by the railroad tracks, and killed and raped her in the snow. He didn't remember killing her either. He said he "dreamed" it, but he gave details about the crime that only the killer himself could have known.

"What do you daydream about, Dewey?"

A killer would seek out some dark warm place in his mind to hide if you let him. Dislodging him if he gets there is like trying to poke a badger out of its hole.

"Dewey?"

He shook himself. *"What?"*

"Tell me about your daydream."

His brow wrinkled. Presently, he said, "I see myself jogging with Suzanne. It's morning. When we get to some bushes, a man jumps out and tries to grab her. I struggle with the man and he tries to choke me too."

His eyes suddenly popped wide.

"Maybe that's why I feel guilty!" he cried. "Maybe I blame myself for not being there with her. I could have saved her."

He was seeking that dark warm place to hide.

"Dewey, you *were* with her that morning."

"I couldn't have!" He clutched his face. "I don't know. *I don't know!"*

I grabbed his shoulders and shook him. "Dewey, let's see it. Tell me about it."

He got still and quiet again. His entire being pleaded with me. "Detective Sasser, I have to know. Please help me. Help me find out if I did it."

Was the man better at this game than I? I thought quickly.

"Dewey, what if I searched your apartment and found evidence?"

He was drifting. "I really thought on that Thursday that I could have killed her," he mused.

"And now?"

"If you find any blood or stuff to show it's me, then I guess I'll have to believe the facts."

I thought I recognized Mr. Hyde daring me to find him.

We drove to Kyle's efficiency apartment. He sat on his bed watching and chatting while I searched the two rooms. I couldn't find as much as a single bloodstain, not even on a towel from where he might have cut himself shaving. He didn't own a pair of black military socks. He wore size-twelve shoes; the footprint at the crime scene was size ten.

Kyle was fastidious, but he did not complain about the mess I made of his place. Discouraged, I stood in the middle of the apartment looking at him. I still had one card left to play.

"Come on," I said.

Kyle followed without protest. I took Riverside Drive and pulled off into the park where a dead tree marked the path down which the killer had dragged Suzanne. A city work crew was clearing out underbrush farther south, but this site would be left intact until I released it.

"Is this where it happened?" Kyle asked, looking around.

Sometimes the murder scene jolted a suspect into confessing. I led the way silently into the thicket. It had rained all morning. A gentle misting rain pattered grayly on green foliage. It absorbed sound. Walking into the tiny ivy-carpeted clearing where Suzanne's body had lain was like walking into a cathedral. The chalk outline of her body had already melted into the wet soil. I noticed the little pulse pounding in Kyle's neck as he glanced about apprehensively.

I stopped on the spot where the killer finished with Suzanne's body and left it. We stood there for nearly an hour in the misting rain while I questioned Dewey Kyle. I probed and twisted and wrenched at him until our hair plastered against our scalps and we blinked from water dribbling into our eyes.

He said, "I want to know as badly as you if I could have gone insane and done something like this. I feel better now. I just don't recognize anything."

"There's one more thing," I said.

Water beaded on his glasses.

"Dewey, look around. Can you show me where Suzanne's body was lying?"

I watched his face. A lot depended on the next minute. He wiped his glasses with a finger. He looked bewildered.

"You're standing on her head!" I snapped.

He instantly sprang into the air and came down six feet away. No one could have faked the horror written on his face. Rain dripped, clicking on leaves, as his eyes riveted on the ground where he had been standing.

LZJ was waiting for me when I returned to the bullpen. I was alone. Johnson licked his fingers nervously and slicked down an imaginary loose hair.

"You let him go?"

I kept walking. I collapsed at my desk. I left wet footprints on the floor.

"Columbo, the Gray Ghost is on my ass."

"Some of these days Kyle'll do one," I said, "but he didn't do this one."

"He *confessed* to his counselor," LZJ argued.

"No," I said. "No."

McCracken looked at me. He looked at the sergeant.

"Leave him alone, Larry," he said. "If Columbo says the man didn't do it, then that's good enough for me."

I kept getting kicked back to the beginning of the case.

The man, if not stopped, will kill again.

CHAPTER TEN

The leaves on the grove of trees where Suzanne Oakley died in the park began to color for autumn. LZJ was hyper because I had exhausted all obvious suspects. Just like Jess McCullough had done with Martin and Rosenbaum. The sergeant licked his fingers and cast reproving looks at me behind my piled-up desk.

"The chief's on my ass," he complained. "He wanted to know how the case was going. Do you know how it makes the sergeant look when he has to tell the chief he doesn't know what his own men are doing? Where's your reports?"

I emptied my pockets. They were filled with scribbled notes on old envelopes and napkins and pieces of yellow legal paper. LZJ stared.

"What's that?"

"My reports."

He stared some more. I got up to walk out.

"Columbo, I'm giving you another week or so. Then I'm gonna have to start assigning you cases again. The killing keeps on."

Two scroungy-looking cocksuckers were waiting in the outer office for Burglary to question them. One had a tattoo on his arm of a donkey humping a woman.

"Maggots," I muttered, and went on out and down the elevator to the police parking lot.

It was just the dead girls and me now. The rest of the squad had to go back to working their own cases when the Oakley leads ran out. I didn't want to believe I had come to a blind alley. Hiking up my baggy trousers, I went back to the beginning and started going from door to door up and down Riverside Drive like an insurance salesman. I canvassed virtually every house and apartment building near the park, then spread out from there into the adjacent residential areas, asking, "Who is strange in the neighborhood? Who is a Peeping Tom? Who has odd sex habits? Who is violent and roams the park? Who is *talking* about the case?"

Asking.

It reminded me of the Margaret Stiles case.

Margaret Stiles was a fat bleached blonde who divorced her white husband and married a northside black, whom she also divorced. Then she started shacking up with any black jitterbug, pimp, or needle hype who would take in her and her three kids. Her escapades ended one spring morning when a junkie neighbor found her stabbed and strangled on the floor of her house next to a place that had rotted out so you could see the rats and mice scurrying around in the crawl space underneath. Her fat ass was broad and bare and stuck up in the air from underneath her nightgown. Cockroaches crawled in and out of her gaping snatch. Doc Roberts looked at it and said, "Look at the barn door on that bitch."

Virtually everyone who knew Margaret Stiles—

black or white, male or female, *even her own mother*—had a motive for killing her. She cuckolded her lovers, rat-holed trick money from her pimp, stole from her mother, beat her kids, lied to everyone. . . . She was more thoroughly despised than any human being had a right to be. Her funeral session lasted ten minutes; all the preacher said about her was that she was born and died and was survived by her mother and brother or somebody and three children.

It was a case in which there were *too damned many suspects.*

That was the thing with the Oakley case and its Martin and Rosenbaum satellites. I had run out of direct, obvious suspects, but there proved to be no shortage of suspects who *might* have done it. If people knew how many freaks in a city were capable of crimes like that, they'd lock and bolt their doors at sunset, chain them, put bars on the windows and Dobermans in the yard, and mount a 60mm recoilless rifle in the living room just in case everything else failed.

The weirdness just kept on and on.

Betty Soiffer told me her boyfriend carried a switchblade knife with a six-inch blade. Everytime he spotted a pretty jogger, he remarked, "There goes the killer's next victim."

Wendy Shaffer had been talking to her neighbor, who confided that her husband went into rages over the slightest thing. He trashed their furniture, beat his wife, and tortured their three-year-old by burning her with lighted cigarettes.

"She says he thinks he's a prophet of God. He really went into a rage when he saw on TV about Suzanne Oakley."

A twenty-six-year-old derelict named Maxwell darted into the street and waved down Detective Bunny Brown.

"I think I might have killed them three girls," he announced happily. "I think I'm Dr. Jekyll."

Brown brought Maxwell to me.

"Everyplace I go," Maxwell said, "I see policemen following me. So I decided it must be because I killed them girls."

Notes, letters, news clippings with messages scribbled on the borders, knives, clubs, packaged clothing crusted with chicken or beef blood—it all kept pouring in.

> Gentlemen:
>
> Frequently when searches are made all over the place, the missing link is found right in one's own backyard. What could be a better place to hide than to be working in your own organization?

I dismissed nothing as a possibility. No one is exempt when it comes to having kinks in sex. I knew a cop who raped his girlfriend's ten-year-old daughter, another we caught in the backseat of a parked patrol car going down on a fag. I questioned a cop about where he was and what he was doing on the morning Suzanne was killed. Like I told Dave Highbarger, the M.E. investigator, the killer could be *anyone*—a cop, a preacher, the corner grocer, a schoolteacher. I interrogated a cross-sampling of Tulsa society, from laborers and skid-row habs to lawyers, politicians, and a TV news commentator.

It seemed a decade ago that I stood in the morgue with Suzanne's body. I had been so confident. I solved difficult cases.

I was no longer so confident.

The killer could be *anyone.*

I kept at it. The weirdness grew.

Marie Rosenbaum's pathetic life and death touched something in a would-be novelist, who decided to write a book about her. The manuscript managed to find its way to my desk:

> Let us bear societies' burden all you people, for we are the labeled human race, yes, we are all the Atlas of this world . . . This story is factual, though parts of it can only be supposed; for who knows the true working of the female, human, emotional mind? This is her story, as she herself could tell it; and only through her death can we know it. Yes, because she herself lived it and died, leaving her presence known only because of the bizarre and tragic way in which she died . . .

An anonymous lovesick suitor left a note on the mailbox for the object of his affections:

> Donna:
>
> I think I know you and I would like to get to really know you better, if you know what I mean. Please, if you are the girl I think you are, please say yes or I'm afraid I'll have to force you or hurt you. Please, if you are under thirty I think you are the one, please. Let's get to know each other. We don't have to go all the way, just to bed and play. Please let me know. Leave note behind green water drain by south end of building in the morning. It could be worth a lot of money to you. Please. I think I love you.

It was *my* note the freak found behind the green water drain. It said: "Go to laundry room at six. Kisses." Guess who was waiting for him in the laundry room?

"Scummy little pervert," I said.

He started to run.

"If you run, I'm afraid I'll have to force you or hurt you," I said.

Uniformed patrolmen were always uncovering freaks and perverts in the field. Their reports found a place on my cluttered desk.

> Mrs. Jones stated she saw two men in ski masks breaking into the house across the street . . . The suspect asked the victim for a drink of water. When she did not respond, he pulled his penis out the leg of his shorts and started to play with it.

My phone rang off its cradle each time Jack Wimer published another of his Jekyll-and-Hyde newspaper articles. It stunned me how many wives and girlfriends out there suspected their men—and the *reasons* why they suspected them.

"Are you Detective Sasser—the one they call Columbo?"

I sighed. "Speaking."

"I think my husband killed those girls."

Not another one.

"What makes you think that?"

"You won't tell him I told you?"

"Trust me."

"Well . . . okay. I had to go to the doctor today. Do you know what he did?"

"How would I know that, ma'am?"

"Oh. I'll tell you. I was having this funny ache down there. I went to the doctor and he removed a sock from it."

"A *what?*"

"A *sock.*"

I blinked. "A sock from *where?*"

"Where do you think?"

"From your . . . ?"

"From my pussy. Sir, if you're making fun of me, I just won't tell you."

"I was just a little surprised," I stammered.

"*You* were surprised."

"Go ahead with your story."

"It's not a story. It's the truth. Do you know how that sock got in me?"

"I'm afraid to guess."

"My husband rammed that sock in me, that's how. I didn't know he done it until it started getting infected."

"Infected?"

"No wonder! It was one of my husband's dirty work socks. Do you know what Walter said when I went home and accused him of being kinky?"

I tried not to laugh.

"He said he would'a stuffed jewelry up my pussy, only he didn't think we had property insurance. Don't you think he might have killed Suzanne Oakley and them others so he could stuff things up inside them?"

Doc Roberts's eyes twinkled mischievously when I told him about it.

"I knew this fag one time whose asshole buddy rammed a vibrator up his bunghole and lost it," he said.

"Yeah?"

"The fag couldn't straighten up. I was in the emergency room at Hillcrest when he tottered in. Sure enough, they took an X ray and found the vibrator. I asked him if he wanted the doctor to take it out or just change batteries."

A bail bondsman handed me a cassette tape he somehow obtained from a client. The dude who made it was wired or something, strung out for a hundred feet. The voice drawled, slurred, mumbled, whispered. I listened to it in my office library at home. It filled the library for an hour. Dianne came in for a moment. She listened, horrified. Then she shuddered and quickly left.

"I love the thought of killing people," intoned the strange voice. "One time I ran into a masochist in California. He asked me to whip him. He had this big, black leather whip. I whipped him. He was screaming and crying, but he begged me not to stop beating him. I beat him till he was almost dead. I thought he was dead, and I enjoyed it. I enjoyed thinking I had killed him. I enjoy the thought of death. It is really strange. . . .

"I went to a Satan ritual one night where the ritual was to sacrifice a human being. The sacrifice was a beautiful girl. All the people were out in the woods. They were all in black robes and standing around chanting. I heard a scream. I saw a man with a dagger standing over a beautiful girl who was naked. The man plunged the dagger to her heart and she was killed. I liked it. We all tasted the blood. We marked our foreheads with blood. Then we had an orgy. . . .

"The pigs arrested me in California. They said I was contributing to delinquency. We were being beautiful. My sister's neighbors were eight and nine years old. The pig world had not spoiled them. They said we were masturbating together. I shot mine all over the little girl. She laughed. . . ."

Thinking my Mr. Hyde might be one of a breed of serial killers like Theodore Bundy or John Wayne Gacy, who traveled around hunting for victims to slaughter, apparently for the thrill of it, I duplicated sheets detailing the circumstances of the murders of my three girls and mailed them to police departments across the nation, hoping the modus operandi might strike a chord of recognition somewhere else. That began a correspondence with other lawmen that filled a special file with accounts of some of the most gruesome crimes known to man.

From Kansas:

Bodies of two female adults and one small boy found in Graham County, Kansas. Victim number one a white female, 19. Shot with shotgun in left side. Undressed and had had sexual intercourse. Possibly forced.

Victim number two a white female, 21. Also undressed. Death caused by two shotgun wounds in the right side. May have had act of sodomy committed upon her.

Victim number three a small boy, 3. Died from exposure. No injuries.

From Norman, Oklahoma:

The victim was apparently surprised while in bed and stabbed with a knife. The wounds began from victim's upper chest, traversing a course to her lower right abdomen. She was then turned on her stomach and knifed repeatedly in the back, from shoulders to buttocks. The victim was then placed on the floor on her stomach and raped. A tampon was removed and left beside her. The assailant then dropped a clean tampon in the toilet, upon which he defecated. He then apparently prepared some cereal and drank water prior to leaving.

From Lufkin, Texas:

Subject shown [in mug shot] was attempting to leave the scene of a burglary where a mannequin had been taken from a display window. Investigation revealed he was responsible for theft of mannequin from a different store a week earlier. First mannequin was found a day later in a rural area. What appeared to be sperm was found in the breast and vaginal areas, and stab wounds were found on the arms, thighs, and center of forehead.

"The chief's on my ass," LZJ fretted. "Put somebody in jail," he said.

Who?

Remote as the chances might be, I pored over the case files, trying to find some connection between the dead girls and their killer or killers. I lugged the files home with me in a big box. I studied the diary Suzanne kept locked with a little key. I thumbed callously through Geraldine's old love letters. I invaded the journals Marie kept on yellow legal paper. I pawed over every photograph, every letter, every document. I pawed through their lives. I saw Geraldine as a little dark-haired girl grinning from the seat of a bicycle. I saw her married and divorced, married and divorced again. I saw her in the crime-scene photographs dead in the closet.

I knew intimate things about them.

Geraldine's periods, for example, were sometimes late. Once, she had sex with a black man. She ate raisin bran for breakfast, with milk but without sugar. She had a hidden birthmark. Sometimes when she was moody she took long, solitary walks in the rain.

Marie Rosenbaum was a frightened little girl behind the makeup and arrogance she acquired as a stripper in her adolescent world of illicit drugs, free sex, and few morals. She looked twenty instead of sixteen, if you didn't notice her frightened blue eyes. I knew her parents were divorced and that she slept with a stuffed panda after she ran away from home. I knew she sometimes crouched with her panda on the floor of the grubby little rented rooms behind the fag bar on Third Street and rocked back and forth while the strung-out creep she lived with and his hype buddies shot up in the next room and sucked weed and said "Yeah, man!" to each other.

When she or her creep needed money, she turned tricks out of Satan's lounge. Sometimes she took them to her apartment. Sometimes she laid them in the backseat of the john's car.

One of her johns I questioned looked at me. "How's I to know she was only sixteen?" he asked. "She could give a head job like she'd been doing it for twenty years."

"Get this low-life scum out of my sight," I said to McCracken.

Suzanne Oakley kept trying to lose weight. That was why she was jogging. She was afraid she would never find anyone she could love and who would love her back. She had never really known her father, who left when she was a child, and from what I heard, her mother had turned into an alcoholic. Suzanne warred constantly with her emotions. She fought with herself over God and the new morality and the sexual revolution. I wondered if anyone else except me knew that she once considered becoming a nun.

I knew the three girls. They were always with me. Sometimes I thought I knew them better than I knew my own wife. Dianne watched me while I brooded over them.

"What are you doing?" she asked sleepily from her side of the bed.

"Thinking."

I sat on the side of the bed, looking out the window and listening to the night noises around the ranch—whippoorwills calling, Storm pawing at his feed trough in the corral, a dog barking at the Whitehead place. I should have been smoking a cigarette, except I didn't smoke. There was a full moon. It bathed the little meadow outside the window in a wonderful soft light. I watched a cottontail making its way toward the barn.

"You're not getting enough sleep," Dianne said.

Like most cops, I moonlighted off-duty jobs to

make ends meet. I taught Criminal Justice three nights a week at American Christian College in Tulsa; I worked security catching shoplifters for Safeway stores; I was up every morning trying to be a writer. A typical day for me started at four A.M. and ended at midnight. Dianne was generally asleep on the sofa by the time I got home, and the boys were in bed.

"You'd better go to bed and get some sleep," Dianne said.

"In a minute."

"The three girls?" she asked.

I didn't say anything.

"Do you want to talk about it?"

I shrugged. She sat up in bed.

"You can talk to me, you know," she persisted.

"Please, Di. Don't start tonight."

She was always on me about it, always trying to get me to open up and talk to her.

"You never talk about your workday like other women's husbands."

In sudden exasperation, I snapped, "What do you want to hear about my workday? Do you want me to tell you about the murder-suicide I worked today? He shot her, then shot himself. There were wads of maggots on the sides of their heads the size of softballs. . . ."

"Oh, God!"

Dianne was a good wife. She took care of the house and our sons. And me too, when I was there. She belonged to the PTA and went to the school Christmas and Easter pageants with David and Michael because I was often working. About the only thing she ever complained about was that I never shared my thoughts and feelings with her.

"I want to know what's happened to you."

You couldn't share my world with anyone who wasn't a cop. It was too dirty. Only another cop was capable of understanding it, and with another cop you didn't have to talk about it. Doc Roberts had a mistress to escape to, and McCracken said his wife Pamela was like Dianne, always prodding and probing at him.

"Chuck, I just want to help you," Dianne said. "I just want you to know you don't have to bear it all alone."

I remained silent, pulling my second skin tight around me. After a while, sitting in the night looking out the window at the moonlight, I said, "Di? Di, I'm sorry."

She had laid back down and turned her back to me. She didn't answer.

"Dianne?"

I wondered if she was really sleeping.

I sat alone on the side of the bed, looking out the window into the soft autumn night.

Thinking about murder.

CHAPTER ELEVEN

LZJ had something on his mind. I figured I knew what it was when he wanted me to ride northside with him to break the sad news to the wife of Charles Rudolph Valentino Larkin that she had become a widow overnight. The Forty-eight Hour Rule on Suzanne Oakley had expired weeks ago. Her name in yesterday's headlines was already becoming potty paper for puppies.

On the way northside, LZJ stopped at a downtown coffee shop that gave free doughnuts and coffee to policemen. Johnson wouldn't pay for anything if there was a way he could get it for free. I waited in the car. He hurried back out with a sackful of jellyfills. He took off from the curb with his cheek puffed out from doughnut like a chipmunk's and another doughnut in his free hand.

"The Gray Ghost is on my ass," he mumbled around chewing. It was a familiar refrain.

"Fill me in on the three girls," he requested.

"They're dead."

"Is that what you want me to tell the chief?"

"He probably knows it."

"Columbo, you're getting to be a wiseass like Doc Roberts. Do you have any new leads?"

I hesitated. We were working our way north along Greenwood Avenue through a black district of falling-down storefronts, moonshine parlors, juke joints, and shotgun shacks with faded fronts and broken-down porches. The government housing projects were farther north.

"I work new leads every day," I said lamely.

"Nothing concrete, though? Just the freaks?"

I had to admit it. "Just the freaks."

He was trying to break it to me gently. Everybody knew I had failed.

"Chuck, you've tried your best. You've given it everything you had."

"It's not over yet," I came back sharply.

"Nobody said it was, Columbo. It's just that the cases keep piling up and I don't have enough men. You can't make a career of the Jekyll-and-Hyde case."

"I haven't given up on it."

"That's why you're the best detective I've got," LZJ said. "You never give up."

"I'll bust it yet, Larry. I'll either bust the goddamn thing or it'll bust me. Something'll come up. *Somebody* out there has to know something. I'll not let that maggot get away with this."

LZJ studied me a second. He chomped down nervously on his doughnut. A squiggle of purple grape jelly squirted out the bottom side and attached itself to his tie.

"Leave it there," I suggested. "Everybody'll think it's a fishing-worm tie tack."

It left a nice stain even after he rubbed it vigorously with a napkin.

He dropped the subject of Jekyll and Hyde as he pulled up in front of a decent-looking house with a white picket fence and a maple tree. The black woman who answered the door had been sleeping. She wore a faded maroon robe. She knew we were cops, since the only other white men who visited this neighborhood were insurance men and welfare workers, and it was too early in the morning for them.

"Charles ain't here," she snapped.

She hadn't heard that a patrolman found Charles sprawled in the center of North Boston Avenue next to his Cadillac with his chest pumped full of lead. It looked like a TND doper ripoff.

LZJ pushed rudely past the woman. "We need to come in a minute," he said. "It's you we need to talk to."

The living room was neatly kept. Mrs. Larkin yawned and pulled the shades to let in the light.

"What Charles did now?" she asked. "What fo' you wants to see him? I works nights. I swear I can't be keepin' up wif' that man of mine."

They broke down if you told them right away, and then you couldn't get a thing out of them.

"When was the last time you saw Charles?" LZJ asked her.

She frowned, but she replied, "I reckon maybe it was six or so yesterday afternoon when I leaves to go to my job. What fo' you wants to know fo'?"

LZJ continued stalling. "Who was Charles with when you saw him last?"

"I think I be callin' my lawyer befo' I be answerin' any mo' questions," she said, digging in. "Where Charles be now? You got him in jail?"

"Lady, believe me, you don't need an attorney," Sergeant Johnson said, glaring to intimidate her. "Was Charles with somebody yesterday?"

She glanced at the telephone, considering it, but then she sighed.

"I see'd this dude Kevin in the car wif' Charles when Charles he come by to get some money from me.

Wha' fo' you aksin' all these questions about my Charles fo'?"

"Did Charles say where he was going?"

"Charles he don't never be tellin' me where he goin'. I don't aks. It ain't none of my truck. Only the good Lord be knowin' where that man be goin'. Now, officer, you tell me where Charles be. You tell me, hear?"

LZJ shrugged. He looked around. Then he said abruptly, "Your husband won't be coming home, lady. He's dead."

Mrs. Charles Rudolph Valentino Larkin exploded into about a thousand pieces. I grabbed her and eased her onto an easy chair before she swooned on the floor. Her head bobbed around like it was attached to a spring. She started moaning and clawing feebly at her face.

LZJ took a look and hurried to the kitchen. I heard water running. When he returned with a wet towel, I stepped aside to let him wash the woman's face. But instead of ministering to her, he stood spread-legged and solid in front of the chair and regarded Mrs. Larkin with a contemptuous look on his face.

He used the wet towel to scrub the jelly stain off his tie.

"Columbo," he said, "I've given you all the time I can on the Jekyll-and-Hyde thing. I'm assigning this Larkin case to you. From now on, you'll work on the girls when you have the spare time."

CHAPTER TWELVE

I told myself the Jekyll-and-Hyde case was no different than any of the dozens of others I had worked. Why should it be different? Your cop's skin either kept the shit off, kept you from being touched, or it got to you and you became like the day-shift Burglary sergeant who often came to work drunk and had to be hustled off somewhere for black coffee before the brass caught him.

"The sarge has been a cop too long," his detectives said. "Nearly thirty years. He's seen too goddamned much. That's why the old fucker drinks his eyeballs out."

You had to get used to it. In Homicide you got used to seeing kids hung by ropes, scalded to death, beaten with hangers, injected with heroin by junkie parents. Little tongues ripped out and genitals cut off. You got used to it. You couldn't solve all the cases, no matter how good you were. There was no Columbo in *real* life. When LZJ started assigning me investigations again, because the killing kept on, I worked them and only delved back into the weirdness of Jekyll and

Hyde whenever a fresh lead showed up. It didn't touch me. It was just another case. Victims were victims.

I was used to it.

I was used to stiffs in airtight rented rooms where the stink of death crept into your hair, your clothing, your mustache, crept up your nostrils and clung to the little hairs.

"What's that horrible odor?" Dianne cried, making a face.

"What odor?"

"It's the most disgusting thing."

I came close for my customary welcome-home peck. Dianne recoiled.

"My God, Chuck. It's *you!*"

There had been a dead man in a basement apartment. The closed-in stench struck me with the fetid breath of hot, putrefying flesh when I opened the door. It must have been 110 degrees inside. Greenhead flies blanketed the window by the door in a droning frenzy. I could hear them over the corpse in one of the back rooms.

I stepped back, closed the door, and sat on the outside steps for a minute, sucking in the fresh outside air. Some people across the street watched me. They had complained about a smell. I stood up and took off my coat and tie.

I held my breath and batted at the flies as I ran through the apartment looking for the stiff. He was in the last bedroom, flat on his back in bed. He must have weighed 300 pounds. The bed sagged in the middle and held the drainage from where he had bloated and split open. A green cloud of flies covered him.

I stared, not wanting to touch the awful thing to check for knife wounds or bullet holes. While I stared, something stirred in the corpse's gaping mouth. Out darted a little mouse.

I've hated mice ever since.

I didn't say anything to Dianne about it. I went in, took a shower and changed. Then I took the dirty clothes out back to the burn barrel by the corral and made a fire. Dianne followed me to talk, away from the boys. She didn't want them exposed to this kind of reality any more than I did.

"Was that somebody dead?" she asked, grimacing.

"Yes."

"It's so horrible. How do you stand it?"

"You learn not to let it bother you."

She looked at me. "How do you learn a thing like that?"

"You learn it."

You could still smell death in the burning clothes. The stallion, Storm, nickered at me from the corral. I started to walk away to greet him.

"Chuck?"

I paused. "When do we eat?" I asked. "I'm hungry."

I was used to it. There would always be murders and murderers. You couldn't solve every goddamn one of them. So what?

An old woman shot between the eyes so her grandson could collect on her life insurance. A store attendant robbed and coldly executed by an ex-convict with six prior felony convictions. Drugs and pimps and thieves and whores and killers like Jekyll and Hyde . . . That was my world away from the ranch and away from Dianne and my sons. You had to let the shit roll off, because if you didn't . . .

I deliberately went out once to kill a man. He had been raping his six-year-old daughter since she was three. Any unexpected sound made her cry out and try to hide. Every man that came near frightened her.

The mother had known about it all along.

I stared. "You mean you kept that baby there with

him even after you found out what he was doing to her?"

"He promised me he'd stop it," she whined.

I went out alone to arrest the father. I didn't want any witnesses. All I could think about was how the rest of that baby's life had been destroyed.

I kicked down his front door, hoping to encourage him to run or to fight. He was a big man and I'm not, but he must have known by the wild look in my eyes. He dropped to his knees and started weeping and blubbering and begging. I shoved my gun muzzle against his head. It would have been so easy. We were the only two in the house. All I had to do was claim a felon resisted arrest. No one else need ever know.

The man started praying.

I couldn't execute a man. My job was to enforce the law, not take it into my own hands.

I brought the man in alive. Then I went off by myself for two days until I could get my thoughts straight again.

"Are you all right, Chuck?"

It seemed Dianne was always asking that.

"Why shouldn't I be all right?"

A "compassionate" judge sentenced the piece of human garbage to six months and suspended that on the condition that he undergo psychological therapy. I heard later the man's wife took him back. I suspect he continued to rape his poor little daughter until she was old enough to run away, get hooked on drugs, or kill herself.

You had to get used to it. Let the shit roll off.

One detective would not eat meat if it were the least raw. Another could not watch his wife sleeping because sleep made her appear dead. Still another, like Jess McCullough, washed his hands every time he got near water.

"Can you smell it?" he asked. "I smell it all the time."

"Smell what?"

"Dead people. I wash my hands, but people still smell it on me."

"I don't smell anything."

I didn't notice it on myself either unless one of the Burglary dicks or somebody got a whiff and said something. Or unless Dianne made a face and stepped back when I started to kiss her. I simply drew my cop's skin tight around me and let the shit roll off while I kept everything else safely inside. I was good at it. I was so good at it that whenever a policewoman friend named Monte Peterson got bogged down, she called me and we went out for pizza or something and I'd let her talk it out.

"Chuck," she always said, "I don't know what I'd do without you. You are my rainbow."

You had to keep the shit from touching you. So they were dead—Geraldine Martin, Marie Rosenbaum, and Suzanne Oakley. I couldn't bring them back, and even when I caught their killer, he faced maybe ten years in prison at the most before he was back out doing it again. Cops knew, goddamnit, that you didn't get emotionally involved, not with your victims, not with anybody. You knew no good could ever come of breaking that rule.

I read a book one time that was supposed to be a true story about a Texas homicide cop investigating the murders of three teenagers. This law enforcement veteran showed up in the woods where the bodies were found. He knelt over the stiffs one by one in an emotional scene and muttered something like, "I don't know how this happened to you or who did it, but I promise he'll pay for it. I give you my word. It's not right and I won't let it happen."

Afterward, the cop burst into tears and pounded his steering wheel and prayed to God: "Lord, it's not right for them to be left dead out there like that. I pray You'll help me find out who did it. . . ."

It was the most disgusting spectacle.

"Why?" Dianne asked. "Just because you're a policeman doesn't mean you can't have compassion."

I scoffed. "If that jerk carried on like that over every murder he worked, he'd be in the rubber-gun squad by now. Or on the looney farm. It'd rot out your insides."

"I think you'd rot faster keeping everything bottled up."

I asked McCracken what he thought about the praying cop.

"Dipshit," he said.

I asked Doc.

"When did you ever see a *real* cop go on like that?" he asked. Doc hesitated. "Still," he said, "there's always at least one case that'll come along and get to you. When that happens, the case'll either make you or it'll break you."

"Did that ever happen to you, Doc?"

I couldn't see anything like that affecting Doc Roberts. Doc was a brick, a boiled-in-the-wool, die-hard, tough guy. Nothing touched him. He even conducted autopsies himself sometimes, under the M.E.'s supervision. That was how he got his nickname "Doc." One day I came upon him at Hillcrest Hospital in the pathologist's office with Dr. Leo Lowbeer, a gnome of a man from Austria. Lowbeer was brilliant too, but you always expected lightning and thunder and Dr. Frankenstein's monster to rise from under his knife. There the two of them were—Doc and Dr. Lowbeer—bent over a corpse split down the middle. Their rubber-gloved hands were elbow deep in blood and guts.

"The sonofabitch has been around dead people *too*

long," McCracken said. "They don't mean anything to him anymore."

"Doc?" I said. "Did it ever happen to you? Did a case ever get to you?"

His cowlick snapped to attention and his eyes hardened into little dark balls.

"Death is the only justice," he said. "The only justice there is comes from the barrel of a cop's gun."

I saw he believed it. Some case *had* got to him.

"We throw killers and thieves in jail, and the courts convict or acquit them on the basis of who has the best lawyer," and Doc was off and going. His eyes just kept getting harder. "But even if some turd *does* get the death penalty, it doesn't mean anything. Do-gooders start screeching and howling about cruel and unusual punishment. They want to *rehabilitate* the maggot. You forget about the real victims after a few days, but the killer—the poor, misunderstood killer—*he* becomes a victim of society. *He* spends about six years in the joint before he's paroled. *He* goes from the death penalty to life to *six* fucking years. That's justice American-style.

"Death," Doc said, obviously thinking of the case that had got to *him*. "Otherwise, there isn't any justice anymore."

Fully half the men on my Homicide shift had killed people in gunfights, a fact that sometimes made LZJ, who hadn't, a bit uncomfortable. Jack Powell shot and killed a doper, I think it was; Harold Harrison shot a burglar; Doc Roberts once killed a car thief; for Bill McCracken it was a bang-away gunfight with an armed robber who was toted off to the morgue afterward; and for me . . . for me it was *Moses*.

Bringing *justice* at the barrel of a cop's gun, like Doc said. Keeping the shit from getting to you.

"It's a goddamn jungle out there," McCracken said. All the cops said it. "It's a sewer. The world is full of nothing but turds and assholes and maggots. Don't trust nobody. Every cocksucker out there'll stab you in the back, lawyers most of all. Nobody gives a dog fuck for the cop. So you don't give a dog fuck for nobody else either. It ain't worth it, letting the shit get to you. Do your job and go home and forget it."

Sometimes, though, when you weren't watching and weren't careful, some of the shit got through to you. I thought of Mrs. Cummings. Only McCracken knew about her and me. "Bingo," he said.

"It's such a lovely day, Chuckie," Mrs. Cummings always began when she telephoned. "Will you come sit with me for a while on the porch?"

She called once or twice a month. I always went, no matter what else I had going.

Her house occupied a place mid-block in one of those gray neighborhoods erected around the time of the Great Depression. The houses were built spare and lean, like the times that generated them. They showed their age. Shingles had fallen off onto lawns that needed manicuring. The house fronts were wrinkled and cracked, like the faces of the old people who hobbled up and down the sidewalks. Mrs. Cummings had lived in the same house for over forty years. She raised kids there; her husband died there.

Now, she was afraid to sit out on her front porch alone.

She peeped through a curtain and unlocked the door only when I started up the rickety porch steps. Then she flung open the door and rushed out to hug me before she brought out lawn chairs and tea and cookies or whatever else she might have baked that morning for my visit. We sat together on her porch when the weather was pleasant and had treats and talked about flowers and books and her grandchildren. She called those days our "special days." She was old and tiny, but her intelligent blue eyes remained as active as a mockingbird in a tree. She retained a fine and inquiring mind even though doctors had been afraid the mugging and assault she endured would leave her impaired. She had been in a coma for two months. She was still not fully recovered.

"Chuckie, you would have liked my husband. You remind me so much of him. Twenty years ago before he died we used to sit out here evenings and . . ."

"Chuckie, have you read James Mason's *The World of Suzie Wong?* It's the most lovely book. When you're not a policeman anymore, I wish you'd write a love story like *Suzie Wong . . .*"

"Chuckie, this whole yard used to be covered with the most beautiful flowers . . ."

Mrs. Cummings talked about everything except the mugging. It happened on a bright June day the summer before Suzanne Oakley, when she'd gone to the Skaggs Store on Twenty-first Street and Memorial Avenue, her old-fashioned black purse with the long strap on it hanging from one shoulder. After she finished her shopping, she came out to walk along the east side of Skaggs to her parked car—a tiny, elderly woman in a little pillbox hat and a long dress.

Two dirtbags came running from behind her. The one in the red shirt and long, greasy blond hair snatched her purse. The long purse strap got caught around her arm. The scumbag jerked her to the sidewalk, where she banged her head. It knocked her unconscious. The punks kicked at the fallen form and slashed her with their fists until the purse finally broke free.

"You fuckin' old bitch! Turn it loose, you whore, or we'll kill you!"

The pieces of garbage laughed with excitement as they ran away with the purse. The old woman sprawled unconscious in the sunshine, blood oozing from her head.

TV was in the middle of a public-service campaign against crime. One of the most frequently aired spots showed a kid stealing a car. Menacing black letters rolled up on the screen as the kid roared off in the car: DON'T MAKE A GOOD KID GO BAD; DON'T LEAVE YOUR KEYS IN YOUR CAR.

Yeah.

DON'T MAKE A GOOD KID GO BAD; DON'T CARRY YOUR PURSE.

Nobody expected the old woman to make it. We worked the case as a homicide. She lay in a coma with the sheets pulled up to her chin and the soft white hospital light blending her pale face and silver hair into her pillow. I stopped by once or twice to look at her. Her nostrils fluttered. I thought it was just a matter of time. I stood by her bed a long time and watched her lying there struggling to live because two teenage thugs thought they had the right to steal her purse.

Her purse had twenty-seven dollars in it. Something like that.

"She just keeps hanging on," I told Dianne. "She should be dead, but she won't die."

Dianne looked at me a long time.

"It's just a job," I said.

I walked away.

"Chuck, I wish you'd think about teaching school."

I caught the punks by working the streets. Somebody finally snitched. The suspects were both seventeen years old. Dopers. They already had juvenile rap sheets for burglary, strong-arm robbery, and narcotics violations.

"She should have let go her purse and she wouldn't

have got hurt," they said when I busted them. "It was her fault."

It was *her* fault!

It was the times. You excused the punks because *society* made them commit crimes. After all, the National Jaycees selected Lloyd Tisi for one of its Ten Outstanding Young Men of America awards. Tisi at the time was serving a life sentence in the joint for a particularly brutal rape-murder. He would have made a good Jekyll-and-Hyde candidate.

Outstanding Young Man of America!

I still can't stand the Jaycees.

The vicious punks who snatched Mrs. Cummings's purse were certified in court to stand trial as adults rather than go through the juvenile system. Their attorney argued that injuring Mrs. Cummings was an "accident." They wouldn't have hurt her if her purse hadn't got caught on her arm. A judge sentenced each of them to one year's *probation.* They were out and strung out on drugs again two weeks after I arrested them.

Doc Roberts grinned. "It makes sense," he said. "Instead of locking them up, we'll have to build walls around ourselves to keep them *out.*"

Mrs. Cummings built that wall around herself when she finally recovered and got out of the hospital. She even canceled her subscription to the morning *World* because she lived alone and was afraid to go out to retrieve the paper off the porch. She had become literally a prisoner in her own house.

Whenever I came for a visit and then left again, she got this wary and hunted look on her face. We had our "special days" together.

Then one day she died in bed with her doors locked and all the windows bolted. Locking herself *in* to keep them *out.*

"Everything's backward and all fucked up," I said.

"It's not right that people are victimized and nothing ever happens to the victimizers."

"That's just the way it is," McCracken said. He was a cynic. "There's really nothing you can do about it."

"We've got to do something. We've *got* to. If not the cops, then *who?* There's nobody else."

CHAPTER THIRTEEN

One impossible whodunit—Jekyll and Hyde—was enough; I didn't need another.

"It's rape-murder," LZJ said. "It might be related to the girls."

The old lady on the floor was getting ripe, even if it was February and cold outside. The gas heat had been left on. The third-floor apartment was like walking into a furnace. Doc Roberts rolled the body over a little to take a look, and the body let out gases, farting and belching. Doc coughed a couple of times, I held my breath, the patrolmen watched through the doorway from outside in the hallway where they could get some fresh air, and LZJ said quickly, "I'm leaving it to you and Doc, Columbo. Put somebody in jail." He hurried out.

"Bastard did this must be a *real* sicko," murmured one of the young uniforms guarding the door.

I gave him a half grin. "Hey, even grannies need loving."

Virginia "Bessie" Sanders, sixty-three, lay belly down on the hardwood floor with her slacks pulled down to her boot tops, baring her bottom, her face turned to one side and the cord off an electrical appliance pulled tight around her neck. A poodle that had been locked up with her over the Valentine's weekend had started licking the feces off her butt and ended up gnawing on the soft places in her face and crotch. Blood and body fluids had leaked out her mouth and dried on the floor.

"Get this fucking cur out of here before I maim it," Doc snarled.

Doc Roberts and I were partners who complemented each other. I liked to step back for an objective look at what I called the Big Picture. People and the crimes they committed were remarkably uncomplicated if you stepped back and looked at them. They were like an oil painting. If you got too close, all you saw were the brush marks and little blobs of color and the flaws. But it all made sense if you stepped back and looked at the Big Picture. You could see the farmhouse and the trees and the road that led through the trees.

Doc, on the other hand, was a detail man. I remembered how Doc pored for hours over a little chip of fireplace brick he found in the carpet next to a man shot through the head. The house appeared to be ransacked; the murder weapon was missing. LZJ and the others were already marking it off as a burglary-murder. Doc just looked and studied and slung his graying cowlick out of his eyes and studied some more. Then he peeked up the fireplace chimney.

"This is no homicide," he announced. "It's a suicide."

The dead man had arranged his suicide to look like a homicide so his wife could collect on his insurance policy. He attached one end of a cut bicycle inner tube to a revolver and the other end inside the fireplace chimney so that when the pistol was fired and released it would be jerked out of sight up the chimney. That was what chipped the brick. Doc was never satisfied with a case until all the details went together.

I painted the panoramas with an all-encompassing wide brush and Doc got down on his hands and knees and put in the detail strokes.

David Highbarger, the M.E. investigator, was eager to initiate our little game. "Well, Columbo?" he said.

I laid out the scenario for him.

Bessie Sanders was probably an alkie. This was the neighborhood for it. It was a dismal place. The downtown rooming houses like the one Bessie lived in attracted welfare people, alkies, dopers, and such because of cheap rent, cheap bars, and cheap cafés. The newspapers would print a little blurb about her on about page five or six—DOWNTOWN WOMAN SLAIN—and then everybody would forget about her because people live forgettable lives in this part of the city. An autopsy later confirmed that Bessie was drunk when she died.

The old woman's body lay clad in high boots and a leather coat over her blouse. All the lights were off in her third-floor apartment.

"She had just come home from somewhere when the assault occurred," I explained to Highbarger.

"Her assailant broke in and was waiting for her to come home?" Highbarger guessed.

"No," I corrected. "He came upstairs *with* her."

"How do you know that?"

I grinned tightly. "We're three floors up. Her killer didn't come through the windows unless he's Spider-Man. Her door lock is not jimmied, and it locks automatically when you close the door. It was locked when Bessie's landlady found the body. That means ol' Bess opened the door *for* her killer—and the door locked behind him when he left. What I'm thinking is Bessie Sanders was a sad, lonely old broad who picked up the wrong Valentine in a bar to bring home with her."

That was the Big Picture. The details were that she had been raped anally, struck on the head, and strangled with the cord off her own toaster. The apartment had not been ransacked, her purse was untouched.

There'd been some speculation at first that Suzanne Oakley had been raped anally.

Doc and I hit the streets. The local barflies and drunks remembered seeing Bessie around on Friday the thirteenth, but for all most of them cared, she could have gone home that night with a six-foot-tall red, white, and blue Easter bunny.

"A lot of people could have killed Bessie," a fry cook said. "She didn't take strangers home with her, but it didn't take her long to get acquainted. Know what I mean?"

"Bessie ran with all kinds of people," added a day laborer who sauntered into the Chaparral Club wearing patched overalls. "Prostitutes, lesbians, dopers. I know. I used to be a junkie. Now, I'm just an alcoholic."

"She was bisexual," recalled a fat barmaid. "I know Bessie went to bed with this one bitch lives in the Alden Apartments. Do you think a lizzy killed Bessie?"

A cabbie took Doc and me for a ride while he talked.

"She was turning tricks," he said. "I wouldn't screw an old cunt like that myself, but lots of other guys did. A hole's a hole in the dark, I guess. Now, some of the guys she tricked were weird. Like, she was telling me about this one who brought two peacock feathers with him. He paid Bessie and this other cunt named Glenda to strip down and stick these feathers in their butts and prance around and around him singing, 'I'm a pretty peacock! I'm a pretty peacock!' while he sat on the floor and jerked off."

We heard a mechanic named Dale Cornwell saw something on Friday night. He lived in a room above a garage. Car engines roared, tools clanged, men cursed, and gas fumes hung so thick Doc was afraid to light the cigarette lodged in his mouth where his tooth was missing. A closet door kept cracking open while we questioned Cornwell. I eased over to it and jerked it open. A stringy-haired little woman with round, startled eyes cringed in the closet among old newspapers and greasy shop rags.

Cornwell jumped up.

"It's all right, fellas. That's just my wife. She's afraid of people. She hides in the closet when somebody comes. Honey, you can come out now. These nice policemen won't hurt you."

She stayed hiding in the closet.

"Sorry I can't help you fellas," Dale Cornwell said. "I just don't remember seeing Bessie Sanders."

The closet door cracked open as we were leaving. One eye watched us suspiciously through the crack. Doc gave the eye a little bow and a grin. "Ma'am," he said. "Nice place you got here."

The trail was already three days cold by the time we picked it up. Forty-eight hours later it was still cold. I went home to the ranch after a shift and left all the shit behind in the city. I worked my horses, went to PTA meetings with Dianne, and took the family out to dinner. Just like ordinary people.

"Why do you always sit with your back to the wall, watching people?" Dianne asked.

"Well . . ."

Officer John Olin in Miami got shot in the back with his own gun.

"Why is it that almost all our friends are policemen and their wives?"

"Well . . . I trust them."

The telephone rang at home. Sergeant Dave Harrison said an old woman named Annie Parks called, saying she knew who killed Bessie Sanders. I got up to leave.

"Your murders?" Dianne asked.

"I won't be long."

"It doesn't matter. The boys and I are used to being alone."

She went back to watching TV.

Annie Parks was slobbering drunk when I found her. Thick makeup flaked off her wrinkled face like dandruff. She took a chair in her ratty room and placed it by the window so she could look down into South Denver Avenue. Through the torn curtain I glimpsed one of the downtown habs stumbling by on the dark street in a flurry of snow. He was bundled deep into an old mackinaw with one sleeve missing.

Annie slowly turned eyes on me that were as pale and rheumy as cheap wine.

"You know Bessie was an alcoholic?" she whispered, and even then her voice sounded loud in the single small room. The light bulb on a long cord from the ceiling made ancient shadows in her face. "I warned her it would lead to trouble. I was right, wasn't I?"

"You were right."

Snow hissed on the windowpanes.

"Time passes . . ." Annie muttered through some great sorrow. "Time passes . . ."

"Annie?" I said.

She shook herself. "You don't want to listen to an old woman," she said.

"Annie, you were going to tell me about Bessie Sanders . . ."

"Yes," she said. "Yes."

I waited.

"Annie?"

"Oh. I—I didn't remember this till last night when I went down to the Chaparral for a drink," she said. "Just one, mind you. We was all in there talking, and there was this one fella—John Blackstock—happened to mention he wasn't even in town the night Bessie was killed. That's a bald-faced lie. I seen John in the bar that night talking to Bessie."

"Are you sure it was the same night?"

"I remember 'cause it was Friday the thirteenth and everybody was talking about it being bad luck. I guess it was bad luck for Bessie all right."

"Did Bessie leave the bar with this guy?"

"I don't know that," Annie said. "I left before she did. I don't normally associate with them kinds of people."

Doc Roberts had his days off, so McCracken went with me running from downtown rooming house to rooming house asking about John Blackstock. To my surprise, late the following afternoon our questioning brought us to a scabby old house right next door to the rooming house apartments where Bessie Sanders lived and died. You could stand on the porch and see Bessie Sanders's window. We checked it out because there was a sign—ROOM FOR RENT—tacked up out front.

"Hard times," explained the talkative old lady who owned the house. "A body can't live on that shitty little check from Social Security, so I rent out two of my rooms. Mr. Blackstock rented one of them about two weeks ago."

"How damn convenient," McCracken muttered, looking at Bessie Sanders's window.

"Mr. Blackstock ain't home right now," the landlady said. "He goes to work about this time and works nights. I don't know where. He ain't did nothing, has he? He seems like such a nice man."

I kept her talking. It wasn't hard. She was starved for someone to talk to. Like this one crusty old woman who told me: "You get old, you get ugly. The United States is a young, pretty people world. They don't want to fuck with you when you get old and ugly. They think you get stupid and have nothing worth saying when you get old. They just want to sweep your warty ass out of the way and act like you ain't even there."

"Wasn't it awful about that woman getting murdered next door?" said Blackstock's landlady. "A body just ain't safe anywheres from sex fiends. Mr. Blackstock and I were talking about it. He said he thought we ought to execute every sex fiend we caught. I thought he might know her, but he said he didn't."

There was one good reason why a man would lie about knowing a murder victim.

"He knocked off the old bitch," McCracken concluded, ready to jump on it.

The next morning when Blackstock came home from work, McCracken and I were lounging on the front porch waiting for him. He was a tall, broad-shouldered man of about fifty with craggy, rough features and salt-and-pepper hair. All the blood drained from his face and he deflated like a flat tire when I flashed my shield. He proclaimed his innocence with a fierce, frightened intensity.

"I didn't kill her. The reason I said I didn't know her was because the newspapers said her name was Virginia. The only thing I knew her by was Bessie. Sure I seen her Friday night, but I thought she was killed the same day you found her dead, and I *was* out of town on Monday night and Tuesday."

"You left the Chaparral with her Friday night," McCracken accused.

"No! Bessie was still sitting there when I left. I'm off work on Friday nights, but I work Saturdays during the day. It was a little after one A.M. when Bessie said to me, 'You're not going to get much sleep.' So I got up and went home."

A polygraph test backed up his story. McCracken rammed his hands deep into his pockets and looked disappointed. LZJ came around.

"Are you going to nail the maggot?" he asked. "The chief was wondering."

"Tell the chief we're going to bust him for felony red light. He has an outstanding traffic warrant."

"Huh?"

Blackstock gave us one thing, though.

"Did you see Bessie talking to anyone else at the bar that night?" I asked.

"There was another man sitting at the bar on the other side of Bessie," Blackstock replied. "He kept interrupting our conversation."

The thing Blackstock recalled most about the other man was that he grinned a lot.

"A weird kind of grin," he said.

CHAPTER FOURTEEN

Doc and I went searching for the guy with the weird grin. We were in the Chaparral taking refuge from the cold when a short, plump woman with hair dyed bright red dropped down at the table with us.

"This guy you're looking for," Betty Henson said. "Maybe I thought of something."

"Lady, I'll buy you a beer," I said.

"Okay. What I seen was, last Friday about midnight I seen Bessie at the bar talking to this man."

Doc looked away, no longer interested.

"John Blackstock?" I guessed.

"It was after John left."

Doc looked back. "Buy her *another* beer," he said.

"I didn't say nothing before because I didn't think anything about it," Betty Henson went on, "but then I got to thinking. Bessie went to the bathroom and came back and said she was going home. This fella jumped up and said he'd walk her home. They acted like they knew each other."

"Who was he?" Doc asked.

"I've seen him around before. He hangs around in

here and around the corner at the Gay Nineties. We haven't none of us seen him all week, though. He don't talk much. He just kind of hunches down at the bar and drinks. He gets this big shit-eating grin on his face when he looks at a woman or when a woman looks at him."

About the red, white, and blue Easter bunny. I had to take that back. Betty Henson *had* paid attention. She described the guy right down to his underwear. He was about fifty or fifty-five, five feet nine, 150 pounds, she said.

"His hair is getting gray and real thin on top. Big ears. I mean *big*. Dumbo ears. He's got little asshole eyes. They sink way back in his head, but his eyeballs bulge and are very round. He's got high cheekbones and the strangest grin."

"So we keep hearing."

"Tell you what," Betty Henson chirped brightly. "My boyfriend is kind of an artist. Maybe Bill can draw the man for you if I tell him what he looks like."

What did we have to lose? Doc and I waited in Betty's seedy little westside apartment while she guided Bill into creating a lopsided caricature of a creature with huge ears, thinning hair, and a "weird" grin all stuck on top of a scrawny chicken's neck. Bill awarded his masterpiece to us with all the pride of having unveiled a Picasso. It even *looked* like a Picasso.

I didn't know what to say, so I murmured, "Remarkable."

"Incredible," Doc echoed with thinly disguised sarcasm.

Betty loyally insisted a professional police artist could not have more faithfully captured the suspect's likeness. "Anybody can recognize him from that picture."

To our continuing surprise, Betty Henson proved correct. People hanging around the Chaparral and the Gay Nineties *did* recognize it. The Homicide detail was a little more difficult to convince. Jack Powell took one look, guffawed, and collapsed with laughter.

"That's our killer," Doc said.

LZJ's eyebrows flew up on his forehead. "Roberts, this better not be another one of your bad jokes."

We received similar responses everywhere we went. Doc and I shuffled into patrol-squad meetings, grinning sheepishly, and handed out copies of the sketch. "We'd like you guys to keep an eye peeled for this character. . . ."

That was about when some patrolman laughed and it all started.

"I saw him Sunday in Dick Tracy's comic strip."

"Are you guys shittin' us or what?"

The sergeants had to step in to restore order. "I thought you detectives had more to do than go around playing with cartoons."

Even the chief ambled through the bullpen with a copy. He dropped it among the debris on my desk and went out, shaking his head and kind of grinning.

It was an odd clue, granted, but it was the one clue we had. Doc and I hit the streets with it, going to downtown taverns, cafés, hotels and employment agencies, showing the grotesque thing to anyone we could collar. Some people laughed, but others recognized it. We picked up a faint trail and followed it like a pair of hounds after a cold fox.

"He comes in here sometimes," said a barmaid at Bowens Lounge.

"What's his name?"

"I never heard it. I haven't seen him around in a couple of weeks."

Someone at Cliff's Club added to that: "He never says nothing to nobody when he comes in. He just stares at women and grins. Everybody calls him the Grinning Hyena."

"That looks like the Grinning Hyena," people said.

The Grinning Hyena.

"You already got a Jekyll and Hyde," Doc noted. "Now a Grinning Hyena. Add a vampire to that and maybe a werewolf or two and you could direct horror films."

The Grinning Hyena's convoluted trail twisted along the fringes of lower-class society and throughout skid row. An obese waitress with yellow sweat rings at her armpits burped, plucked a roach out of a sugar bowl and stomped it, then studied our sketch.

"Whatta ya want him for?" she asked suspiciously.

"Income tax evasion," Doc said.

"He oughta get a medal is what, keepin' money away from them fuckin' politicians."

"How about murder?"

"Oh. He the one done in that ol' broad on Denver Avenue?"

"Could be."

"Why didn't ya say so? The farthead's name is Jim. That's all I know. He worked here one day washin' dishes, then he quit."

We kept hitting the flophouses and bars, wearing out shoe leather.

"He's a cook at the Post Café," someone said.

The fry cook at the Post resembled old Gorgeous George the wrestler.

"He don't work here no more. I got him as a dishwasher from the State Employment Office. He worked two days and quit."

"Do you know his full name?"

"I might have lost his application."

Gorgeous George sorted through a stack of papers soiled with grease and ketchup and eggs and stuff.

"I don't have it. He kept talking about how he just

got out of prison for killing some fella in a barfight. Wait a minute. Here it is. Name's Jim Walsh. If anybody could look like that picture you got, it's him. Ugliest fella I ever seen."

The police computer kicked out of the files the name James Walter Walsh, age fifty-four. His mug shot *did* resemble the Grinning Hyena sketch. His rap sheet was enlightening. Doc and I skimmed over the dozen burglary arrests and the like and got down to his last conviction—a thirty-year sentence for manslaughter. It hadn't been a man in a barfight he killed. It was a *woman.* The Corrections Department released him on parole about a year ago, about the time Geraldine Martin, the first of my girls, was murdered.

We dragged out the old crime file on a woman named Dorothy Clark, whose body was found thirteen years ago facedown in her bedroom on South St. Louis Avenue. She had been stabbed twenty-five times and beaten with a claw hammer. Captain Bob "Smokey" Stover, now head of Police Intelligence, had worked the homicide. He said the stiff was left fully clothed but exposed from midriff to knees, just like Bessie Sanders. Dorothy Clark had also been raped—anally.

"A guy told us Walsh was AC-DC," Stover said.

Dorothy Clark met Jim Walsh at the downtown Tulsa Arena Club, only a few blocks north of the present Chaparral Club. They left the bar together late at night and walked to Dorothy's little house a short distance away, where Walsh attacked her. The Sanders murder was almost an exact replay of the Clark homicide thirteen years earlier.

I shook my head.

"Why can't we keep these dirtbags in jail where they belong?"

"Don't look at it that way," Doc admonished.

"Look at it as job security for us. It makes sure we always have something to do."

LZJ expressed amazement that Doc and I managed to track down the Grinning Hyena with our Dick Tracy caricature. He slicked down his hair, shook his head, and walked off.

"Put somebody in jail," he said.

That was easy after we tagged the Grinning Hyena with a real name. Two days later we snatched Walsh out of the State Employment Office where he was waiting meekly in the unemployment line. I looked at the little scrote. It seemed he'd jump out of his skin if you said boo at him. Blackheads bubbled out of a face the color of cooling lava. Ash filled the crevices in his skin. He kept grinning for no reason. His grin *was* the humorless grimace of a hungry but cowardly hyena.

There is an old saying in police work that the guilty have the best alibis. Innocent people don't remember where they were or what they were doing at a specific time two weeks or a month before.

"I went to Bowens Lounge after I got off work," Walsh recited. "I drank beer until it closed at midnight. Then I walked around to the Chaparral where I had one beer. Then I went home. If Bessie was even there, I didn't see her. The last time I seen her was in November when I went to her apartment with her and had two beers. That was the only time I've ever been to her apartment."

If the man looked like a hyena, he was also as wily as one. His statement covered himself should we have found his fingerprints in Bessie's apartment. He didn't have to do that. There were no fingerprints. Oddly enough, there was also not a scrap of other physical evidence—no hairs, blood samples, shoe marks—nothing we could use to prove James Walsh had ever intruded across the dead woman's threshold.

Putrefaction and the idiot poodle eating on the body had destroyed most everything.

Betty Sue Henson pointed out Walsh in a lineup—"That's him. That's the Grinning Hyena!"—but it still proved nothing. Even if Walsh left the Chaparral with Bessie, it didn't prove he killed her.

"You killed Dorothy Clark the same way," Doc Roberts accused.

"They said I done it, but I didn't do that one either."

Like always, I cross-checked each sex criminal against the Jekyll-and-Hyde case. It turned out Walsh was paroled *after* the Martin murder, and he had a good alibi for the morning Suzanne Oakley went jogging for the last time. He had been working. Doc Roberts looked frustrated. We were going to have to spring the man for lack of evidence. He killed old Bessie Sanders, but he was going to walk on it.

"Friday the thirteenth was Bessie's unlucky day," Doc told him. "Jim, you're going to find out it was yours too."

The man was con-wise.

"I already had my say. I ain't got nothing else to tell you."

I went upstairs to the jail and peered through the bars at him in the holding cell. He fidgeted and grinned. I came back the next morning and studied him again. Walsh grinned some more. Uneasily. He might be cunning, but I guessed correctly that he wasn't exceptionally bright.

Maybe there was a way. Part of my reputation as a good homicide detective was based on the unorthodox methods I used to crack a case. LZJ was always bringing up the time I set up the socialite as bait for a robbery. It worked and we caught the robbers, but it made the Gray Ghost so nervous he nearly became a real ghost.

I handed Walsh a pack of cigarettes through the bars.

"What's that for?" he demanded, but he snatched the cigarettes out of my hand.

"Nothing, Jim," I replied in an understanding tone. "I saw you were out. One pack is certainly not enough to repay you for the two days we've had you in jail."

He nodded, looking put-upon.

The theory of social reciprocity says that if you give something to someone, he feels obligated to give you something in return.

"Jim, if you're telling the truth about not killing old Bessie, then I need your help."

Put that way, how could he refuse? He jumped eagerly off his bunk.

"Jim, you seem to have good intelligence and a sharp memory. It's important that I know exactly what Bessie was wearing that Friday night when you saw her at the Chaparral."

I made it sound like we were merely continuing a conversation started previously. Walsh's eyes squinted. He scratched his head. Hadn't he told us he *did not* see Bessie that night? I frowned impatiently. He *owed* me for that pack of cigarettes.

It worked.

He said, "The best I can remember, she was wearing red or maroon slacks with a dark leather coat."

I almost whooped. The scumbag couldn't remember from last time exactly what he told us.

I pressed on. "Where was she sitting at the bar when you saw her?"

"I don't remember," he snapped. "I didn't leave with her. She was still sitting at the bar when I left. I didn't even talk to her that night."

When the cell door opened, the Grinning Hyena departed the station house in such a hurry that he was practically hopping up and down with nervousness and relief. Doc and I grinned at each other. LZJ blinked suspiciously.

"What're you up to this time, Columbo?" he asked. "You're up to something. I can tell. You'll give the chief a heart attack."

CHAPTER FIFTEEN

I doubted if the Grinning Hyena had a conscience, so Doc and I settled for paranoia. For the next several weeks, in between following Jekyll-and-Hyde leads, which I never neglected, and pulling in the strings on a Mohawk Park homicide in which a rendezvous between two fags ended with one dead, Doc and I perfected a devious little game that had as its objective making Jim Walsh see things that go bump in the night.

It started out with one of us, either Doc or I, driving by either where Walsh lived or worked two or three times a week and merely waving at him, making sure he saw us. It was the oldest detective gambit in the business. It didn't take long for the man's grin to wear thin. He started moving around to different rooming houses, trying to escape us, but we always found him. He would come out of his lair one morning and look up and down the streets for us, and, sure enough, there we'd be. He telephoned his parole officer complaining that policemen were following him day and night wherever he went. We heard it got where he couldn't sleep. One night he jumped up and stalked from window to window with a long-bladed butcher knife.

"Goddamnit, I know you're out there. Leave me alone! *Leave me alone!*"

He developed a nervous tic in his eye. He lost weight until more and more he resembled the gaunt, haunted caricature in the sketch Bill drew of him.

Doc and I kept driving by, waving and smiling.

"When will you close the case?" LZJ demanded.

"When we can get a conviction."

"The chief's on my ass about it."

"You got plenty of ass to go around."

On March 28, six weeks after the Sanders murder, Walsh moved into a rundown westside duplex with a half-wit woman and her blind poodle. On March 29 there was a rap on his door. All the blood drained from his lava-gray face when he found Doc and me on his porch smiling at him.

"We need your help again, Jim," Doc opened.

Walsh was so nervous he stuttered. "I—I don't have nothing else to say."

"You know your rights, of course," I said, shrugging nonchalantly. "You don't have to talk to us. Is there something you're trying to hide?"

Quickly: "I ain't hiding nothing."

"Then why won't you help us?"

He looked trapped.

"We want you to show us which apartment Bessie took you to," I proceeded.

"I didn't go anywhere near her apartment!"

"We weren't talking about on Valentine's, Jim," Doc said. "We were talking about when you walked her home that night last November, remember?"

"How's that gonna help?" he demanded.

"It's detective procedure," I explained. "We're trying to find out if anything has changed in her apartment from when you were there until the night somebody killed her."

"Oh."

He wanted no part of the cops, but we left him no easy way out. He was so overwrought by the time we stopped in front of the tall dreary building off Denver Avenue that his Adam's apple bobbed furiously from his efforts to swallow. We climbed the stairs and I unlocked Bessie's door. I watched with some amusement when we stepped inside and Walsh's eyes darted everywhere around the room *except* where we found the old woman dead. His eyes avoided that spot as though afraid her ghost might rise in front of him.

"Did you know her goddamned dog was starting to eat her?" Doc commented in casual conversation.

Walsh's heart pounded in his temples. His eyes rolled back. Doc's eyes brightened. He enjoyed cat-and-mouse games.

"Oh, one other thing, Jim . . ." I ventured casually, again as though continuing a former conversation. "What time did you say it was when you and Bessie left the Chaparral that night she was killed?"

Looking confused, he wet his lips and his mean little eyes shifted around.

"I didn't go to her apartment," he protested.

"But you left the club with her. That's what you told us."

"I did?"

"Jim, you're not going to start trying to lie to us?"

"No! No!"

He took a deep breath, thought about things a minute, looking pained, and then said haltingly, "It was after midnight, I guess. We might have walked out of the club at the same time, but I went one direction and she went the other. I crossed Eleventh Street and went home. She was walking toward the Gay Nineties the last I seen of her."

One more step.

As Walsh was scrambling out of our car in front of his duplex, I dropped another bomb on him.

"Jim, you noticed, didn't you, how the windows in Bessie's apartment overlook that vacant lot across the street?"

Walsh blinked and frowned.

"Jim, you've been a big help to us and I want to let you in on something. We may be getting a big break. We've learned there were two fags parked in that vacant lot the night Bessie was strangled. We think they saw who did it. As soon as we find them, we'll know who the killer is."

The Grinning Hyena almost fainted. His lips moved but no words came out. He hurried mutely to his door like something was pursuing him. Doc got to chuckling so hard tears rolled down his cheek.

"Poor little cocksucker," he said. "Maybe he'll have a coronary and save everybody a lot of trouble."

Sergeant Johnson kept inquiring at morning squad meetings: "What are you two doing about your morgue of unsolved cases? What about Bessie Sanders?"

"We're setting a trap," I said.

"Oh, God!"

"Nothing elaborate this time," Doc said. "Just two fruits and a blind poodle."

LZJ stared.

"I'm not going to ask," he said. "I don't want to know. Just put somebody in jail."

On May 10, nearly three months after the Sanders murder, Doc and I parked our unmarked in an alley down the block from Walsh's duplex to watch another step of our scheme unfold. Two undercover vice cops, Don Bell and Charley Jackson, swished onto Walsh's porch and knocked on the door. They had been carefully coached.

"Are you Jim Walsh?" Bell asked, affecting a mannerism and a slight lisp.

"What do you want?"

"Now, sweetheart, don't take that attitude," Bell purred. "You're bringing down a lot of heat on us. The pigs is already looking for my friend on warrants. We don't need the kind of heat you're bringing us just because we seen you through the window with that dead woman."

Walsh grabbed the doorjamb and hung on.

"You didn't tell them anything, did you?" Walsh cried when he was able to speak.

"No, man, whatta you think we are, snitches?" Jackson put in. "It ain't none of our business as long as you can make it right with us."

"Yeah, yeah," Walsh muttered quickly. "Don't say nothing to the police. I'll pay you money. Anything. Just don't talk to the cops."

"Now you're talking," Bell said. "We don't like the fucking pigs any better than you do. Maybe that old cunt deserved killing. Killing is about all them old whores are good for."

"Just don't say nothing."

"You got it. We'll be in touch."

Doc laughed for two days. "That stupid little cocksucker," he said.

Naturally, we couldn't use Walsh's admissions in court, since it was entrapment. If something ever came up about the "two queers," Doc and I would blink and make a joke. Who'd ever believe such a preposterous tale?

Three days later we were back at Walsh's door. Walsh looked like his brain needed a jump start.

"You look awful," Doc said to the Grinning Hyena. "Have you been getting enough sleep?"

We used the same old scam—we needed his help, and left him no way to refuse without appearing guilty. Back we sped to Bessie's apartment. We stood around the dark stain on the hardwood floor where Bessie had bled. Walsh couldn't help staring at it this time.

"The cord ruptured her larynx and made her bleed out the mouth," Doc explained.

Walsh flinched. He kept staring at the bloodstain.

"Now," I began, "how long did you say you were inside here when you walked her home on Valentine's?"

Walsh wrenched his eyes from the floor. He replied slowly, doubtfully, "The only time I came here was in November."

My brows shot up in feigned surprise.

"What's wrong with you, Jim?" I snapped. "You told us last month that she was afraid and you walked her home."

"I did?"

"Do you have something wrong with your memory?" Doc asked.

Walsh started to tremble.

"Damnit, Jim, stop changing your story on us!" I cried. "You want us to think you did it?"

"I guess I forgot," Walsh apologized.

"Then how long were you here?"

He took a deep uncertain breath. "I guess I forgot because I was only here a minute," he said finally. "I stepped just inside the door, then I said good-bye and left. That's all there was to it."

He dug in. He would only go so far at a time. I steered him to the windows overlooking the vacant lot across the street. The unmarked was parked there. I pointed.

"That's where the two queers were parked when they saw you through the window," I said.

Walsh gasped. *"Me?"*

"Oh. Did I say that? I meant to say, when they saw *whoever* killed Bessie."

Walsh's brain went into a coma. He uttered not another word for the rest of the time we had him.

"When?" LZJ persisted.

"Before Christmas," I said.

May 25 was a lovely spring morning with a great sun when Don Bell, alone, rapped on Walsh's door. Doc and I watched expectantly from our alley. The next hour would tell whether our scheme of the past three months worked or whether it fell to shit and the Grinning Hyena walked for good on Bessie Sanders's murder.

"The pigs busted my friend last night," Bell told Walsh. "Look, sweetheart, he's telling the police everything about how we seen you kill that old woman. I'm getting out of town. What you do is up to you, but I don't want to get mixed up in this bullshit."

Bell departed in a hurry. Doc and I waited, watching. It didn't take long. Walsh's door cracked ten minutes later and his head shot out to take a furtive look up and down the street. We knew the man had broken under the strain.

"Now we play catch up," Doc said.

Walsh hurried out of the house carrying two big cardboard boxes. The half-wit woman he lived with followed carrying another box and leading the blind poodle who fell off the porch and then ran into a tree. Walsh's head swiveled nervously back and forth on its skinny chicken's neck. Man, woman, and dog rushed to the car parked at the curb and piled into it with the boxes.

They were getting out of town fast.

Doc and I still waited. The collapse was more complete if you let them glimpse freedom before jerking it out from underneath them. We waited until the car started pulling away from the curb. Then we swept down on the Grinning Hyena like gangbusters. Doc blocked Walsh's car with our unmarked while I jumped out, pulled Walsh from his car, threw him across the hood and handcuffed him.

It was all for effect, for drama, a way of letting Walsh know we meant business this time because we had the witness. The blind poodle and the half-wit added to it by yapping and screaming and crying in all directions. Walsh's body slumped in on itself.

The Grinning Hyena had no grins left.

An assistant D.A. called Doc and me over to his office and said the Sanders case was entirely circumstantial even with the admissions we wrung out of Walsh after his arrest. He said circumstantial cases were time-consuming and expensive to try.

"He's fifty-four years old," the assistant D.A. reasoned. "The Public Defender will cop him to a plea of manslaughter. That means the state revokes his parole on the other manslaughter. That's as good as a life sentence."

"He's a perverted little creep," I said. "He bungholes women he kills because he learned to like it in prison where there are no women. He's killed twice. He'll kill again if he's ever released."

"Oh, by the way. Do you guys know anything about two homosexual witnesses the P.D. keeps talking about?"

Doc and I looked at each other.

"There are no witnesses," I said.

District Judge Robert Green accepted the plea bargain. He sentenced James Walsh to serve four years in the state penitentiary.

It stunned me. *"Four* years?"

"He'll have to serve his eighteen-year parole revocation before he even starts on the four years," the assistant D.A. explained.

That was what he said, but that wasn't what happened. Less than two years later Walsh received *another* parole. Two months after that, the sex-crimes detail busted a James Walsh as a suspect in the rape and assault of a middle-aged woman near a downtown bar. Doc and I went up to the jail to see if it was really the Grinning Hyena.

"Get them out of here!" Walsh screamed when he spotted us. "Make them go! I ain't saying a word to them!"

"Justice!" Doc Roberts scoffed. His eyes hardened into little dark balls. "Ain't no such thing as justice. Lady Justice isn't only blind—she's deaf and dumb and mentally retarded. Everytime you look, the system has her cranked over and throwing the meat to her."

Walsh's rape victim couldn't identify him at his trial. Grinning, he hurried out of the courtroom.

About eight months passed before we heard of the Grinning Hyena again. Police in Iowa found a murdered woman lying facedown and nude from the midriff to the ankles. The last we heard, James Walsh had been convicted of that one and was a suspect in two others over in Ohio or somewhere. He's supposed to be serving life in prison now.

I wouldn't bet on it, though.

CHAPTER SIXTEEN

Whodunits like the Grinning Hyena case popped up for me again and again as the weeks and then the months passed. Like Doc said, the killings kept on. I solved most of them. Yet, like Doc also said, there were times that one case got to you. For me, it was Jekyll and Hyde. I couldn't completely explain why. Maybe it was because of the fact that the victims were three attractive young women, all snatched off the street and destroyed in such an appalling manner. Maybe it was simply the fact that catching the pervert had become a personal challenge.

Whatever it was, all the others in the world might go free, but I wanted that one single killer to face *justice.*

I received calls from as far away as California and Florida and New York, from homicide cops with whodunits of their own. They were looking for clues too, seeking to link my Jekyll-and-Hyde murders and their unsolved ones to some Gypsy serial killer. In Nebraska a girl had been kidnapped and murdered. When the police found her, her vagina had been cut out and the slayer had apparently taken it with him. A freak in Texas drove all over the state with a woman's head in his car trunk. A character in California knifed his mother to death and then butchered her, literally, cutting her up into ribs and loins and steaks and such to serve his guests.

Sometimes I felt like a central clearinghouse for bizarre unsolved murders. Anytime one surfaced in Oklahoma, no matter where, some detective was bound to telephone.

"Call that Tulsa cop Sasser," they suggested. "He's got files on all the weirdos."

"It's been over a year since we read about the last Jekyll-and-Hyde homicide," a Kansas policeman said. "Are you ever going to give up on it?"

"I'll catch him," I said. "Someday."

On a cold, damp day a week before Christmas I got out of my unmarked on a rural county road not far from where we found Marie Rosenbaum's body. There were sheriff's deputies and state agents all over the place. It was out of Tulsa's jurisdiction, but someone suggested calling me. The dampness seeped through my old black trench coat. I shivered and drew it tight around me. I went up to look at the corpse tossed in the mud alongside the road.

Partial corpse, rather.

It was a woman with the head, arms, and legs missing from the joints nearest the torso. The body had been stabbed nine times with a long-bladed knife. But there was no blood anywhere. It was like the body had been drained somewhere else before being dumped here. The M.E. had to grind up some flesh like hamburger in order to obtain a blood type.

McCracken stared.

Rain had been weeping from a low sky for the past week, making a sea of mud around the corpse. With all that mud, there should have been the killer's footprints. But everything around the corpse was smooth and undisturbed. It looked as though the Jane

Doe had somehow been gently placed on top of the mud about twenty feet from the road. If she had been dropped from a helicopter or airplane, she would have at least made an indention in the ground.

"Damnedest thing I've ever seen," someone muttered.

"Well, Columbo?" M.E. Investigator David Highbarger said, trying to start our little game. "How do you explain this?"

"I can't," I said, stunned.

McCracken glanced wryly at the sky. He was still thinking about it a week later at a party we attended with our wives.

"Sasser ain't looking for no Jekyll and Hyde," he declared.

As usual, we cops at the party formed a little clique of our own and the noncops got together in another corner. Cops told each other funny stories about the streets—about gunfights and chases and pimps and one-legged whores and dead bodies. That sort of thing. Some of the noncops kept hearing the waves of coarse laughter and intense conversation and drifted over to see what was happening. Dianne cast me a warning look from the women's circle, but I had had a couple of drinks and felt loose.

"There wasn't anything but that trunk in the mud and no way it could have got there except by air," McCracken went on. The noncops looked at him with rounded eyes. "All the blood was *sucked* out of it. No arms, no legs, no head, the blood sucked out, and just laid there on top of the mud real gentle. You figure it."

"Who did it?" a noncop asked, arriving at the end of the story.

McCracken was drinking bourbon and felt a little loose himself. He looked at the intruder.

"We have a description," he said, looking serious. "It's a very pale white man about six feet tall, last seen wearing a black tuxedo, bow tie, and a black silk cape."

"That's unusual dress for a murderer, isn't it?" the noncop asked, looking puzzled.

"Not for this one it isn't," McCracken said, passing it to me.

"We've put out an APB. The guy flies a lot," I added.

"Can't you catch him at the airports, then?"

"He doesn't use them. The only thing we have is a first name and an M.O.—Dracula, and he sucks blood."

The cops guffawed at the noncop's expense.

"They fit his baggage easier when he travels if they don't have all those appendages hanging from them," a Burglary cop cracked. "Sorta like taking a cool one for the road."

The civilians were horrified.

"How can you guys *laugh* about things like that?"

Bill McCracken nudged me. We had them going. "Partner, tell them about poking your finger in that broad's hole."

I laughed. "It was just a little hole."

"Tell it, Columbo."

I glanced around. Dianne was still casting me cool glances.

"This broad got shot in Comanche Manor," I said. Comanche Manor was a black northside housing project. "I was just down the street and heard the gunshots. About four million aborigines came charging out carrying this broad by her arms and legs. Blood pumped two feet in the air from the bullet hole in her forehead every time her heart beat. She was dying. There wasn't a damn thing I could do about it, but the natives wouldn't accept that. They started getting nasty. 'Muthafucka honky gonna let this girl die an' ain't doin' nothin'.' So . . ."

"So he did what any lusty young cop would do," McCracken finished with his scarred grin. "He stuck his finger in her hole."

"It satisfied the natives," I said, adding, "That was the only time I ever had a broad die on me with my finger in her hole."

The noncops looked uncomfortable. They watched us laughing for a minute like we weren't quite human. One of them was an accountant whose closest contact with our world was the TV news and "Kojak"; he was a guy with a pale face and watery eyes that made you think he was always looking at his mother.

"This is why we still have a Jekyll and Hyde running loose killing women in Tulsa," he said snippily. "The cops don't take their job seriously enough to catch him."

McCracken described it later: it was like someone farted in church. A couple of cops turned their backs and started other conversations. McCracken watched me. Dianne was looking too. I stepped close to the guy.

"You don't know what the fuck you're talking about," I said, grinding it out.

The guy got red in the face, but he looked around at the circle of hard, silent faces with the streets written in them, and he quickly decamped. He and the other civilians resumed telling their own stories about how absolutely *horrid* it was what Angela said to Robert when they accidentally met at a party with their new spouses. We cops kept in our own world of fags and gunmen and dead OD'd dopers stinking up motel rooms.

"Oh, Chuck!" Dianne sighed on the way home.

I kept driving.

"You didn't have to do *that,"* she cried. "You ruined the party."

That was far enough.

"*I* ruined the party? That little sonofabitch gets in my face and tells me I don't take my job seriously. For a year I've busted my ass on that case. Goddamnit, I *live* with that case!"

I couldn't see them in the darkness, but I knew there were tears in Dianne's eyes. We couldn't even talk about my work without it ending like this.

"I know you live with it," she said. "You live with death and violence all the time. That's all you think about—*murder*. I watch you sitting in the library with those boxes of reports, thinking about murder."

"I might have missed something in them."

"You're missing something all right. You're not the same. It's not just the Jekyll-and-Hyde case. It's the job."

"The streets don't touch me," I said. "I don't let them."

I felt I had to deny it. Sometimes I looked in the mirror and saw a stranger with the cop's characteristic tightness around the eyes and a gaze as hard and suspicious as a cornered wolf's. I wasn't even thirty-five years old, but in many ways I was ancient. I was older than any man my age ought to be and still remain alive.

For some reason it struck me earlier that night how much I had aged. I was standing at the mirror shaving for the party when something triggered a flashback. I realized with a start that the kid with the big grin and the zoot suit who became a Miami cop had vanished, replaced by this hard-faced stranger. I stood in front of the mirror, frowning, trying to remember my first days as a cop.

I had arrived in Miami in the early spring that year with eight dollars in my faded jeans and all my worldly possessions lashed onto the back of an 80cc

Yamaha motorbike. I'd ridden the bike for a year, living in a tent, vagabonding it across the U.S. after I got discharged from the Navy in Seattle. I rented a room at The Fowler House, a skid-row rooming house just across the street from what, then, was known as the Central Negro District, a black ghetto, and started looking for a job. The first thing I saw in the newspaper was a full-page ad for the Miami police. The city needed cops; it had the highest crime rate in the nation. Sounded exciting. If you had to work steady, it was better to have a glamour job like fighting crime and evil than being stuck beind some desk. I took the Civil Service exam and came out on the top of the list.

The rooms at The Fowler House were occupied by an odd assortment of alcoholics, day laborers, and old people who could not afford a better place. It was about what you could expect that near the railroad tracks, the black ghetto, and a bumper chroming factory. My room was six feet wide, ten long, and furnished with one twin bed and a dresser with sagging cardboard drawers. The rent was six dollars a week; I rented it on credit pending my first paycheck.

Everybody at the house came around to offer advice on how to pass the various police tests, boards, and interviews.

"Goddamnit, dress nice," counseled Grace, the housekeeper. She was a chunky Italian who kept her gray roots dyed jet-black and her tongue sharpened with curses and four-letter words. "Policemen are conservative bastards," she said. "So be conservative, you little prick. Nothing flashy or shitty. Wear a suit."

I didn't own a suit and I was almost broke, so I went to a Salvation Army outlet and bought a suit for two dollars. I selected a gray one because Grace said gray was conservative. I put it on the day of my oral review board and Grace made sure my tie was on straight. I'd borrowed the tie.

"You are a good-looking little sonofabitch," she said.

The roomful of captains and majors and assistant chiefs fell into a stunned silence when I walked in. They stared at me standing in front of them staring back. What was the matter? Didn't all their applicants appear in dress suits?

Finally, somebody cleared his throat so loudly I flinched.

"Say, boy, where'd you get that suit?"

It never occurred to me to lie about it. I was a mountain boy from the hills of Oklahoma and Arkansas raised to tell the truth, look a man straight in the eye, and keep your word when you gave it.

"Salvation Army, sir."

There I was, a skinny kid with short curly hair, a big honest backwoods grin, and a gray *zoot suit* that had somehow survived the Roarin' Twenties in somebody's closet. It had shoulder pads that filled a doorway, lapels as wide as a desk top, and baggy trousers with big pleats.

Everyone laughed so hard the secretary from next door stuck her head inside the room to see what was going on. She looked at me and laughed too. I laughed along with them, although I wasn't quite sure *why* we were laughing. The oral board was supposed to take fifteen minutes; I was in there an hour. I knew I had passed.

Sometimes Training Officer McFann at the Miami Police Academy made me wish I hadn't passed. He was so *strike* we rookie cadets figured he starched his jockstrap. He didn't even sweat when he climbed into the Bear Pit for "dirty fighting." Officer McFann would have made a great Marine D.I.; maybe he had been one.

That was before police departments started putting women in patrol cars. Women were useful as jail matrons, detectives' secretaries, radio dispatchers, and good to look at in the offices around the station, but the *real* work of fighting crime took a man. As long as Officer McFann was at the police academy, he personally saw to it that no wimps, sissies, or anyone who so much as took a whiff of quiche ever pinned on a Miami police badge.

"Gil de Rubio!" he would bellow into the face of a cadet standing rigidly at attention. His jaw jutted and his ice-blue eyes froze you in your shoes. "What's a cow, Gil de Rubio?"

The response was ritualistic: "Sir, a cow is a four-legged, lactating mammal of the bovine species with . . ."

If the response was one word off, or if you hesitated one beat too long, or if you didn't belt it out like you had a big set of balls, then you went down for push-ups. Or you ran a mile, or you went through the confidence course, or, worse yet, you got into the Bear Pit to fight all 240 pounds of romping, stomping, Nebraska-fed Cuddles. "Don't be a puss. He's just a rookie too. Get in there and *get* him!"

If you survived Cuddles, you had to run some more or stand at attention in your little khaki uniform.

"I don't wanna see one eyeball click, you understand, rook? Indecision can get you killed. I don't give a damn if my rookies are shot by jealous husbands or die of heart attacks, but you're not going to be killed in the streets because that would reflect on me. Do you understand? I am going to make a man out of you. A police*man*. A police*man* is tough. The shit can't get to a police*man*. A police*man* is at *war!* In the streets you are *The Man!*"

I graduated from the Miami Police Academy second overall in the class, first in "dirty fighting." Officer McFann said I'd make a damned good cop, and Grace was bursting with pride.

"Get out there an' give 'em hell," she advised. "You gotta remember, though, that it's us little people that ain't got nothin' an' nobody that needs police most to protect us. Remember that, you little bastard, or I'll come an' kick your ass."

The other rookies had wives and girlfriends and family to come to graduation ceremonies to see the chief pin badges on our new uniforms. All I had were the residents of The Fowler House, but the rooming house was empty on graduation night. Drunk or sober, in wheelchairs or limping on canes, unshaven and maybe a little ripe from lack of bathing, cursing like Grace or silently and impulsively nodding like Walt, they all showed up to occupy an entire row at the police auditorium. The other guests left the row in front of them and the one behind them vacant, but my friends didn't seem to notice. Chief Headley, who, of course, knew about the zoot suit and one of his rookies living in a skid-row rooming house, made a special effort to shake the hands of my odd guests who came to the ceremonies.

They were all so proud of me.

I took to the streets with my big gun and badge. I sincerely believed my calling was a noble one—to serve and protect and uphold the law and ensure justice. I believed in black-and-white concepts of good and evil. There were no gray areas. Not then. It was easy to tell the good guys from the bad guys. *We* were the good guys. We would always be noble guardians of justice in the streets, standing above and beyond what we experienced, objectively maintaining law and order.

It wasn't to be that simple.

Miami was logging the highest crime rates in the nation. For reasons better left to the analyses of sociologists, much of that crime, especially violent crime, occurred in the black slums of Liberty City and the Central Negro District. I was assigned to a "salt-and-pepper" team. A salt-and-pepper team was a white cop and a black cop riding together. It was an experimental project at the time, designed to help defuse ghetto violence.

Some cops called the ghetto "Combat Alley." Others called it "The Zoo." Burglaries, robberies, shootings, and knifings were common. Police patrol cars left parked and unguarded were sometimes burned. Other cruisers occasionally had their tires flattened by gunshots. Dudes in the projects dropped concrete blocks on policemen and their cars. Revolutionary graffiti showed up everywhere:

BLACK POWER

OFF THE PIGS

MY MAN IS STRONGER THAN SAMSON—HE CAN WHIP FIVE COPS

"It's a war going on in them mean streets," a black cop named Vic Butler used to say. "The war'll kill you too if you don't watch out."

One night my partner Charles Daniels and I were pinned down in the stairwell of a ramshackle rooming house by a junkie armed with a .25 auto. He kept cracking open his door and popping off at us with his little pistol. *Pop! Pop! Pop!* Like that. Then he'd slip inside, slip in another clip, and try it again.

In between clips we charged. The door opened a crack and the pistol thrust out at us, pointing directly at my chest. By some miracle the junkie failed to pull the trigger. He darted back inside.

Daniels blew a hole the size of a man's head through the door with his shotgun. There was an awful scream.

A moment later the .25 appeared through the hole in the door, held by two fingers. The dude was ready to give up.

There was still screaming from inside. A woman. She had been lying up in bed drunk. One of the pellets from Daniels's buckshot round had neatly blown off her little toe.

Vic Butler shook his head when he heard of the shooting.

"I hear you almost bought the farm last night," he said. "You'd better remember what I told you if you want to live long enough to collect your medals."

"It *felt* like war," I conceded.

"It *is* war," he said.

Shortly after that I shot off a dude's top lip. A freak shot at an armed fleeing felon who was going to shoot me. No teeth, no nose, just lip. The other cops started making bets on which part of the human anatomy Daniels or I would get next.

The cops had their casualties too. Four of my policemen friends were gunned down; three of them died.

Officer John Olin was shot in a Miami café for no other reason than he was a cop; "social revolutionaries" lured a twenty-one-year-old rookie into a trap and placed a rifle round through his skull; motorcycle officer Ron McLeod surprised an armed robber who shot him point-blank in the face; the old-timer Vic Butler, who had fought his "war" for nearly twenty years, was ambushed in Liberty City and his body riddled with gunshots. His attackers continued to pump bullets into him long after he was dead.

Life in the streets became a series of interconnecting blocks of uncertainty, of never knowing from minute to minute exactly what the next would bring, of hours of routine patrol followed by sudden stark terror. I discovered that crime to the street cop was not some formless and faceless entity, as it was to much of the rest of the country. Crime was *real;* criminals were *real.* Their existence was always there in the background of your mind, and when they appeared they appeared suddenly and with terrible presence.

After a while civilization began to lose meaning. I developed that cop's skin to keep the shit off. You tried not to be affected by the tragedies, crimes, and foibles of mankind. You became a soldier in battle who shut out the sights and sounds of battle lest you also go mad.

The world was made up of two types of people—cops, and then all the rest.

Only another policeman understood what it was like to walk into a dark warehouse knowing that an armed thief might be waiting to blow you away. Your guts shriveled up and died inside your belly; your intestines, which are supposed to be twenty-eight feet long, got so short the bottom opening ended up lodged in your throat. You were scared, but you did whatever was necessary. It was your job.

Memories of the different occasions when I tasted the other end of my gut in my throat piled up in my brain like old rotted pieces of wood:

A pair of gunmen opening fire on me, and I came out with my gun so fast I shot out a mortuary window before I could bead in on them; exchanging gunshots with an armed robber during a high-speed car chase; fighting a rapist toe to toe alone in a back alley; a demented woman holding my partner and me hostage for an hour while we tried to talk her out of her cocked revolver.

I remembered dark alleys, even darker warehouses

where burglars hid; high-speed car chases; being shot at, stabbed at with a butcher knife; the times I was carted off to the hospital for various wounds and injuries; and one night I flung open a door expecting an armed fugitive behind it and began emptying my revolver into a flock of pigeons that rose noisily from the roof.

And I remembered kids hung by ropes, scalded to death in bathtubs, beaten with clothes hangers, injected with heroin by junkie parents, little tongues ripped out and genitals cut off. Stiffs dead in airtight rented rooms in August. The pimp who shot at me sentenced to six months *probation.* A store attendant robbed and coldly executed by an ex-con with six prior felony convictions. Drugs and pimps and thieves and cowards and whores and . . . on and on.

"Why the hell do we do this?" cops sometimes asked each other.

Maybe it was simply because it was a war in the streets and somebody had to fight it.

"You have that cop's skin around you that you're always talking about," Dianne cried, "but it's getting holes in it."

"Dianne, I'm a cop. It's more than what I do; it's what I *am.*"

"Oh, I understand that real well. You said you'd quit if it ever started getting to you."

"I have to do what I have to do."

It got where I didn't want to go home. Home for me became the police station. The other homicide dicks understood—Sergeant LZJ and McCracken and Doc Roberts and Curt Hanks and Bunny Brown and Powell and Bobby Morrison. They understood. I didn't have to justify myself and explain to them why I was the way I was. They accepted me faceup as a damned good cop and a tough one. They even admired me for it.

Sometimes they were more like my family than the real family at home that I was always trying to protect from this side of my life.

CHAPTER SEVENTEEN

Everyone called South Peoria Avenue the Restless Ribbon because of the hordes of teenagers who hung out there on Friday and Saturday nights getting drunk and blowing weed and trashing the parking lots. The Restless Ribbon paralleled the lower end of Riverside Drive. Anything that happened there, because of its proximity to River Park, caught my attention.

One afternoon a tall man who was not a teenager startled a young woman at an apartment complex by sidling up to her after she parked her car. He had wild eyes surrounded by lots of white.

"Have you heard about the murdered girl on Riverside Drive?" the stranger asked abruptly.

Pam Jones blinked, uneasy. "Well . . . yes."

A mysterious smile swept the man's face. Pam shuddered.

"You know I'm the one who did it," he said. "I went to Heaven to get the knife to do it with."

He turned nonchalantly and walked off, disappearing. Pam bolted to her telephone to call the police. LZJ handed me the patrolman's report the next morning. He looked disapprovingly at my desk with its head-high piles of reports, mug shots, and evidentiary debris from old murder and assault cases—a bloody jacket, a knife with a broken point, a jar filled with dopers' addresses, ski masks, clubs and bludgeons, and other odds and ends buried so deeply that after a while I even forgot what was there.

"The chief wants you to clean up your desk," LZJ said.

I reached for the reports in LZJ's hand. "Another freak?"

"This one confessed," LZJ said. "Put somebody in jail."

Pam Jones described her stranger as a man of about thirty-five with a Brillo pad of curly black hair and those wild gray eyes. I rose from my desk, jerked on my jacket, and hitched up my pants. The whodunit I was working at the time could wait.

"Clean up your desk first," LZJ said.

"Later," I shot back over my shoulder.

I never did. There were more important things.

Searching for Pam Jones's stranger was like the Grinning Hyena all over again, only this time I didn't even have the Dick Tracy cartoon caricature. I stumped the Restless Ribbon trying to sniff him out. I checked mental institutions, jail and prison records, welfare and unemployment offices.

"You think it might be *him* this time?" Jack Wimer the reporter asked.

"How the fuck should I know?" I snapped back. "Wimer, I see one word of this in print and Hillcrest Hospital'll be removing your typewriter from a particular part of your anatomy."

"The human race has terminal weirdness," Doc Roberts said.

A few days after the stranger in the apartment complex, a forty-page collection of lunatic ravings found its way to the top of the heap on my desk. The author had delivered the tome to a secretary at Oral Roberts University. It and a song titled "Wild Fog" were dedicated to "free love angel Suzanne Oakley, for real."

> There is more joy in one sinner than in 99 saints. I believe Heaven is free love. What about devoted couples on this earth? The husband won't know his wife because we will all be spirits. What you accomplish here on this world has to work in the far off now. I ask myself (and I mean this respectfully) was Christ never married? Was he a man's man? Could you say he ran around with boys? What about the girls? Did he love girls? They are brides in Heaven. I don't think a man is a bride . . . This whole thing started by me trying to write a song of free love. I now have the strangest feeling I should tear this paper up. Fear rejection . . . .

On and on. It was signed Foxf.

"Foxf?" LZJ said.

"It's probably a code name for one of Oral's ministers," Doc said.

Suzanne Oakley had attended ORU, and Reverend Arthur Manis taught there. Nosing around for background had burrowed me into the inner workings of the beautiful South Tulsa campus with its giant praying hands and spires uplifted to the Glory of God, into "True Seed Faith" and all that. It disgusted me how the foundation solicited tithings from old ladies on Social Security, from the poor, the desperate, the lonely, the ill, all hoping to reserve a harp in the afterlife. They mailed in scabs and pus and falling-out hair to be prayed over. Apparently, the more money you sent in, the more you could expect from God and Oral. "For a five dollar donation," went the content of one solicitation, "Oral will pray over your letter; for ten dollars he will pray over it personally in the Prayer Tower."

"The guy just walked in and handed me the stuff and walked out again," the ORU secretary told me. "He was tall with curly black hair and the strangest-looking eyes."

A couple of days later Foxf returned to ORU to deliver another manuscript. It was a rewrite of his first, with one shocking addition:

> I'll even say I killed Suzanne Oakley with a knife sent from Heaven. Now I used to cry a lot. I mean, really cry a whole lot. Well, I'm not crying now. I've done something. The truth will set me free. . . .
>
> My friends call me Crazy Bobby and God is my mouthpiece. I'm going fishing . . .
>
> Love, Bobby Mitrick (Foxf)

The secretary's description of this "Foxf" and the part about the knife sent from Heaven confirmed what I already suspected. Pam Jones's stranger and the ORU visiting author were the same headcase. McCracken was ready to jump on it.

"My God, partner," he cried excitedly. "I think you're on to Mr. Hyde. He's wanting to get caught. He even left his name and address."

I didn't say anything. I would know the killer when I talked to him.

"Take Miller with you," LZJ ordered.

Jim Miller was a new detective on the detail. I looked at Johnson. LZJ shrugged.

"He needs to learn," he said.

A tall rawboned man wearing thick lenses answered my knock at a door in a small apartment unit on the Restless Ribbon. He peered myopically at the shield I thrust at him, then stepped quickly outside onto his little door stoop and looked suspiciously all around.

"I've been expecting you," he whispered, ushering us inside. "Don't let anybody see you."

He gave me his hand. I shook it cautiously.

"I'm Foxf from Heaven," he announced.

Jim Miller stared.

"You can call me Wild Fog," Crazy Bobby the Foxf said.

I sighed. Terminal weirdness.

Crazy Bobby brushed some marijuana crumbs off his dinette table onto the filthy carpet. He pulled up a chair, sat on it and folded his arms in front of him after motioning me to take the chair opposite him. Miller took a neutral chair. He sat in such a way that his sport coat hung loose and away from the butt of his revolver.

Bobby smiled. Only his lips smiled. His irises behind his glasses resembled hollow caves.

"God sent you," Crazy Bobby said. "You've come about my song 'Wild Fog.' You want to hear me sing it."

Sometimes, with the really weird ones, you had to smash your way through to them.

"I want to talk about murder," I lashed out, watching him for a reaction.

There was none.

"But first," he said happily, "I want you to hear 'Wild Fog' from its source."

"No. We need to talk about Suzanne Oakley."

Bobby's strange eyes narrowed. "You can call me God," he said. "Foxf translated means God."

I stared. I shrugged. "Okay. If you're really God, you'll know what happened to Suzanne Oakley."

Miller was staring at both of us.

"I know what happened to Suzanne," Foxf said. "God and I are one."

I'd had talks with George Patton and Marilyn Monroe and at least two Adolf Hitlers and a Jesus Christ or two, but Crazy Bobby was my first God.

"I'll sing my song first," Foxf decided. "I have a real talent. You'll see."

"Sing the fucking song, then," I muttered.

"What?"

"I'm eager to hear it. Sing."

"The song is dedicated to Suzanne Oakley."

I jumped on the opening. "Why?"

"I can't tell you that. Don't rush me. It took me seven days to create the world."

"Six," I corrected. "You rested on the seventh."

Crazy Bobby glared from his mad caves. I eased back from the table. Then, suddenly, Foxf was beaming with restored good humor. Miller and I watched spellbound as the man's big hands rose slowly from the table and gracefully arced above his head. He began to sing in a not unpleasant baritone.

"You're sure a wild, wild fog
  that's hard to believe.
She sings her song so wild, so free.
  She's free!
She sings her song that's there for me.
She gets down, down down,
She gets down, down down.
Wild, wild fog.
Wild, wild fog, throw out the devil in me.
Throw his ass in the fiery pits of Hell.
Throw his ass in the fiery pits of Hell.
Wild, wild fog."

It continued like that for a half-dozen more verses. Then it ended. Crazy Bobby stared. I clapped my hands twice.

"I'm going to publish it in a song book of inspirational verse," Foxf decided.

"I don't see how the world can wait. Bobby, look—"

"I *told* you. I'm God."

I paused.

"God, will you talk to me about Suzanne?"

God pondered. He looked wise. Finally, he said, "Suzanne is not dead. I saw Suzanne in Heaven."

Now we were getting down to it. I leaned across the table to lock him in on me.

"Did you speak to her?" I asked.

The way he cocked his head and listened to voices somewhere reminded me of another lunatic named Jack Lazar. Lazar had been waiting years in the State Hospital at Vinita for some judge to declare him sane enough to stand trial for murdering a telephone operator. He was still so spaced out that the last time he appeared in court for a hearing he sat massaging his crotch with both hands and making crazy eyes at the court reporter in her low-cut summer dress.

"Bring him back next year," the judge decided.

Was Crazy Bobby the Foxf another Jack Lazar?

"Suzanne's happy," Crazy Bobby said. "Her soul did not like it here."

I kept him going.

"Her soul can't be happy," I countered. "Not when it knows what happened to her here on earth."

"She did not mind being killed. It was with a knife sent from Heaven."

Patience, I counseled myself, sighing.

"It hurt her," I persisted. "What does she want done to the man who hurt her? Can you tell me that?"

He thought about it.

"She wants him brought to God," he decided.

All *right.*

"Can you help me, Bobby?"

"He is one of my creatures. I do not want him harmed."

"He will not be harmed. How do I find out who he is?"

Foxf tossed me a smug grin. "You're the detective," he said.

Who was fucking with whose mind?

"Did *you* do it?" I asked, keeping my tone conversational.

Crazy Bobby said, "I might even say I killed her. That's why I dedicated my song to her. You might say it. Then again you might not."

This nut, this Foxf, *this* was my Mr. Hyde?

"How did you accomplish this, God?"

"Yes, I *am* God," Crazy Bobby said.

Another few minutes. My mind was racing, my heart thumping. It had been a long time coming, but now it was almost anticlimactic. Murderers always seemed larger than life, more evil than evil, until you caught them. Then you were disappointed to find they were nothing but warped little people with rotted cores. You couldn't tell them apart from anyone else on the streets.

I mustn't appear too eager. I mustn't scare him off now.

"How did you take her, God? I'd like to know."

"It was with a knife sent from Heaven."

I waited.

"Actually, it was with a sword," he corrected. "I lay the sword from Heaven on her shoulder and asked her to follow me. I showed her the way through the wild, wild fog to her source."

I kept probing, gently.

"Where did you meet Suzanne?"

"In Heaven, of course," Crazy Bobby snapped. "Suzanne is such a pretty girl. God is free love and Suzanne is my free love angel. I have always liked long red hair."

Suzanne was a short-cropped brunette.

"What was Suzanne doing when you met her?"

"She was jogging in Heaven. Do you want me to tell you about it?"

He did. I began to slump in my chair. The color and length of Suzanne's hair was not the only fact Crazy Bobby had wrong about the case; the only thing he had *right* was her name. I kept at him until I was sure, until I grew brusque from disappointment. He was just another grandiose idiot wandering madly about in his wild fog, bumping into things. Finally I shoved back my chair and stood up. Jim Miller watched, confused by it all. Crazy Bobby sprang to his feet. He threw up his hands a second time and began singing yet another verse of his "Wild Fog."

Miller followed me to the door. I slammed it behind us.

"He didn't do it," I growled. "He's just another fucking nut."

The singing stopped. The voice from beyond the door got in a parting shot.

"Same goes for you!" Crazy Bobby said.

For the next month or two Crazy Bobby the Foxf delivered his Oral Roberts letters directly to me at the police station rather than frightening Oral's secretary with them.

"You're getting them all anyhow," he explained.

I endured them, and him, until he wired Oral's car with a fake bomb in a shoe box. That was going too far. I busted him and held him for a sanity hearing. A district court judge ruled he wasn't insane and let him go. What else could you expect from a lawyer?

CHAPTER EIGHTEEN

It seemed the whole world was turned upside down. It wasn't just the Jekyll-and-Hyde killer, although I wanted him so badly I lay awake nights imagining myself cornering him somewhere in the city. When I became a cop, I believed in Truth and Justice and the American Way. And in Santa Claus and the Easter Bunny and in the Tooth Fairy too, I suppose. Disillusionment had become terminal.

"There is good and there is evil in the world," I tried to explain to Dianne. "There is *supposed* to be justice. We're *supposed* to reap what we sow."

"All you see is the bad," Dianne replied. "That's all you think there is."

It wasn't just me, was it? The world *was* upside down.

I came out of the courtroom where a district court jury had just returned with the death penalty for a punk killer named Michael Wayne Brown. Brown's only reaction was a half sneer as the bailiff led him away. Outside in the hallway I found myself cornered by one of those ever-present advocates for the abolishment of the death penalty. They all had the same cookie-cutter look about them—wimpy, stooped shoulders from carrying around all that liberal guilt, puppy-dog eyes.

"How can you be a party to sending a young man to the death chamber?" the activist demanded with all the self-righteousness of that particular breed of do-gooder.

A sign used to hang in the shift lieutenant's office. It said: GOD PROTECT US FROM ALL THE GOOD THE DO-GOODERS DO.

"He could be rehabilitated and transformed into a useful citizen," the wimp went on. "He has his whole life ahead of him."

I glared at the man.

"The victim had his whole life ahead of him," I countered.

"But he's dead, and revenge against this youngster won't bring him back. Our responsibility now lies toward that kid. He's as much a victim as the person he killed."

I stared. The world was turned upside down.

"Remember Richard Sullivan?" I said. "He used to be alive. Richard Sullivan was the victim. That kid is *not* the victim."

Richard Sullivan was an insurance salesman who stopped by his office late one night to pick up some papers. His wife and teenage daughter waited in the car for him.

"We heard what sounded like a trash-can lid slamming," the wife said. Her eyes were red from crying, but you had to ask your questions anyhow. "When he didn't come back outside, we looked through the window and saw him lying facedown in the hall."

He had been shot once in the back between his shoulder blades. Crime Scene Search found an ejected .22-caliber cartridge casing in the shag carpeting near the victim's feet. The casing told us he had been shot with an automatic pistol at close range. Not close enough to leave scorching and powder on his white shirt, but still close.

"Well, Columbo?" David Highbarger asked.

I went along with the game.

"Elementary," I said.

Highbarger's brows lifted.

"Kids," I said.

"Kids?"

"Kids."

He blinked. "*Kids* shot that man in the back? Executed him?"

"Vicious little kids," I affirmed.

"I'm listening."

"Let's go outside first."

The M.E. office and morgue always smelled like rotting flesh.

It was a pleasant morning in mid-May. It was still cool, with the breezes off the river and a wonderful bright sun. A lone chrysanthemum, white and pure, blossomed in the alley next to the M.E.'s back door. I looked at it. Ordinarily, no flowers grew near this place. Highbarger listened as I ran down the facts for him.

"The perpetrators broke in through a back window and rifled through all the desk drawers," I said. "They were looking for petty cash. That's all you'll find in most insurance offices, if that. There was one of those gag tin cans sealed up with a five-dollar bill inside. The burglars mangled the can trying to get it open. Kids do burglaries like this one."

"Kids," Highbarger said, shaking his head.

That was my Big Picture. *Parents, Do You Know Where Your Kids Are Tonight?*

I took a map of the city and taped it to the glass

window that made a wall next to my desk. The detectives' stenographer's office was on the other side of the glass. The Gray Ghost walked by and shook his head over the clutter on my desk that now appeared to be creeping up the walls toward the ceiling, but he didn't say anything. On the map I placed colored pins to show all the businesses burglarized in the vicinity of Sullivan's insurance office during the past two months. The map was studded with pins—over a hundred of them. The place next door—Stringer Nursery—had been hit four times since the first of the year, also by kids. Burglars had broken into virtually every business in the little shopping center around the corner on Twenty-first Street. Three guns had been stolen from the pastor's office of the church one block behind the insurance office—a .380 Lama automatic, a .22 Ruger auto, and a .22 S&W auto.

"The ejection marks on the death cartridge could have been made by a Smith and Wesson," firearms expert Richard Raska told me.

I went to work putting pressure on the young punks in the neighborhoods and rousting out snitches like Sammy Spider. Spider was eighteen with a long, slim weasel's body, stubby legs, and a malignant growth in the middle of his face that served as a nose. I found a marijuana roach on him one night and let him go. That's how snitches are born. Pathetic little cocksucker. He'd kiss a dog's ass just to get some recognition.

"The only dudes I know doin' break-ins right now is Harley Shaffer and Wayne Paulson," Spider said. "But they don't never carry no gun."

"What do you have on them, Sammy? I need a hammer."

He led me to an old abandoned barn in a grove of persimmon saplings behind a hayfield near Bird Creek outside city limits. There was a stolen Ford inside the barn. It had been stripped of everything except the doors and engine block.

"I was with Harley Shaffer when he stole it," Sammy Spider admitted.

Shaffer was a punk teenager with a Nazi earring.

"I ain't no fuckin' snitch," he protested.

"You are now, you scum-sucking little creep. You got three weeks to come up with a killer's name before I go to the District Attorney about that stolen Ford. With your track record, he'll certify you as an adult for trial and ship your ass to the joint."

It wasn't textbook, but that was the way you did it anyhow. Chief Purdie once remarked, "Sasser solves murders. I don't *want* to know how he does it."

Take a stick and poke it into a hornet's nest and something is bound to come out of it. After I jailed about a dozen petty burglars and car thieves, the rest of the punks got the message I was serious. They started standing in line to snitch in order to get the heat off. They even called me at home nights.

"Where are you going?" Dianne asked sleepily.

"I have to see somebody."

"You've been working late almost every day. Now they're calling you at midnight."

"I'll make it up to you. Now go on back to sleep."

"Chuck . . . ?"

"Yeah?"

She lifted up on one elbow in bed. She lay back down and turned over.

"Nothing," she said.

Two weeks after the trash-can lid slamming, a kid called Sucklip telephoned and met me in Woodward Park. He said he had overheard two boys talking about the insurance man.

"Know what I mean? They was talkin'. I heard they stole some guns from a church. They just got back from California where they been ever since that man got shot. Know what I mean? I heard them talkin'. The short one that looks like that TV guy Baretta says to the tall blond one, he goes, 'The police is gonna think we killed that insurance man 'cause we're doin' all the burglaries.' That's perzackly how he goes. Know what I mean?"

"They're our killers," McCracken said, always ready to jump.

Even LZJ played duck on a june bug. "Columbo, drag those thieving little murderers in here and make 'em talk."

The two young burglars' names were Billy Gilkey and Glenn Dutton. Gilkey was seventeen; he hadn't so much as a speeding ticket. Dutton had had one traffic ticket. He was eighteen. McCracken and I found Gilkey at home on a shady, tree-lined street where mothers in robes and house shoes and curlers called to each other door to door and tricycles were left on the sidewalks. He was a gentle-looking kid with reddish-blond hair and blue eyes. He looked like someone you wouldn't mind seeing escort your daughter to the school prom. I thought he was going to faint when I flashed my shield and McCracken grabbed him and handcuffed his hands behind.

"You're under arrest for burglary and as a suspect in murder," I snapped before reading him his rights.

The courts ruled a cop couldn't question a juvenile —anyone under eighteen—outside the presence of his parents or a lawyer, but that didn't mean you couldn't *listen.* You would have had to gag the boy to keep him from talking as we drove to police headquarters.

"We broke into some places!" he cried. "But I swear we ain't killed anybody. We don't know nothing about the insurance man."

I looked at McCracken. "How did he know which murder we were referring to?"

I could talk to my partner about anything I wanted, couldn't I? So what if it was in front of the juvenile suspect? It was a charade, but the first thing a lawyer would tell him was give name, rank, and serial number, nothing else. The Supreme Court was overthrowing convictions on the grounds that a lawyer who permitted his client to talk to the police was incompetent.

"I read the papers," Gilkey interrupted desperately. "It's all over the streets that Glenn and me killed the insurance man. I ain't got the guts to kill nobody."

The kid was wired. I couldn't question him, but I kept him going with judicious remarks to my partner. By the time we eased onto the downtown police parking lot, the boy had copped to eleven burglaries, all of them within a few blocks radius of the murder site. I could take some more colored pins off my map. He dug in, though, on the church burglary during which the three guns were stolen. He denied that one vehemently.

"That's because he *knows* one of those guns is the murder weapon," McCracken concluded.

I booked Gilkey into juvenile detention for burglary with a hold order for murder. LZJ told Major Sollars I had solved the insurance man's case.

Glenn Dutton was next. McCracken and I staked out his ratty blue Lincoln in the parking lot of a print shop on South Atlanta Avenue, where he worked. I wanted to bust him out of the auto in order to have a legal reason to search when I impounded it. One thing you could say about Bill McCracken—the guy had infinite patience. He could sit for hours and never move more than his cigarette to his lips and back.

Dutton, with his short legs, barrel body, and black hair, really did resemble Baretta. His face dropped to the sidewalk when he came out of the print shop and McCracken and I stopped him from driving off. In the Lincoln's glove compartment I found a partial box of .22 ammunition and a crude pencil drawing on notebook paper of two automatic pistols. Dutton sweated. His trembling rattled the handcuffs and made the detective car vibrate.

Instead of my Miranda warning turning him off—"You have the right to remain silent . . ."—it switched him on like a tape recorder. I let him play. He confessed to everything he had ever done wrong in his life, from swiping a comic book when he was six to busting into an appliance store on Twenty-first Street. He copped to all the burglaries Gilkey copped to, and then some more. But he wouldn't cop to the insurance office burglary that got Sullivan executed, and he denied the church burglary.

"The only gun I got is a shotgun," he said, "and it ain't stolen."

He claimed the .22 ammunition and the sketch of the automatic pistols belonged to his cousin in California.

"He left that stuff in the car when we was out there last month."

I also booked him for burglary with a hold order for murder. LZJ was worried, and he slicked down his hair.

"If you don't come up with more evidence, the D.A.'s going to have to let those kids out," he said. "All you got hard on them is burglary."

"Yeah."

"Do something. I told the chief you solved the case. He's back on my ass again."

Doc Roberts grinned his mischievous grin. "Larry, looks like you got plenty of ass to go around."

The squad was always telling LZJ that.

* * *

I kept pounding the streets. It looked like the pieces were falling into place when I collared the manager of the Twenty-first Street recreation center. I loaded the trunk and backseat of my unmarked with stolen property he had been purchasing from the young burglars who hung around his rec center playing fuss ball and smoking pot. He gave me names. There were so many of them that there was always a line of parents outside the police Juvenile Bureau trying to get their kids out of detention.

The manager told me Gilkey and Dutton tried to sell him three guns they stole from a church. He wouldn't buy them, although he fenced about everything else. And then one of the kiddie burglars the manager ratted on came up with a surprise. He knew Gilkey and Dutton too. He said the pair had been trying to buy guns the previous November in order to rob an elderly local storekeep.

"What are you going to do, kill him?" the pair was asked.

Gilkey the prom boy was the one who responded: "If we have to, we will."

I was glad I didn't *have* a daughter.

Confronted with this new evidence, my pair of teenage suspects confessed to the church burglary but still denied killing Richard Sullivan. I teletyped California police to pick up the stolen guns from Dutton's cousin in Los Angeles and ship them to me for ballistics comparison with the death bullet and ejected cartridge casing.

Dutton looked up at me. He had been staring at his hands in his lap. His hands lay open, like dead birds.

"Mr. Sasser . . . ?"

Sometimes a full confession came like this at the last moment.

"Mr. Sasser, you're a tough man, but you have to believe I ain't killed nobody. Me and Gilkey couldn't do that. We didn't tell you about the church because we was afraid you'd think we was the ones kilt Mr. Sullivan."

The kid was crying. Tears ran down his cheeks.

"Fuck him," I muttered, slamming the interrogation room door behind me.

I cleared a place on top of my desk where I could prop my feet. LZJ was ebullient.

"You got 'em cold, Columbo!" he chortled. "I'll tell the chief."

There were only two pins left in my map stuck on the window. I pulled out the red pin that represented the church burglary. That left one pin. The insurance office. It was represented by a black pin.

Doc Roberts shambled by in his baggy suit.

"Doc, do you ever have little voices trying to tell you something?" I asked him.

Roberts's eyes brightened. "I busted a killer one time complained his hammer spoke to him. He said his hammer told him to beat his wife to death. He said his hammer was psychotic. Now, *you're* hearing voices."

"Fuck you, Doc," I said.

"It's more'n I'm getting at home."

"Doc, everything points toward those kids . . ."

"But you're hearing voices telling you they didn't do it?"

I grinned and stood up. "I'm hearing voices. But don't worry, Roberts. I don't even have a hammer."

McCracken scratched his head and shrugged when the ballistics comparisons came in. None of the church burglary guns was used to slay Richard Sullivan. McCracken had been so sure we had the killers. I blinked and pondered it. Nearly a month had passed since Sullivan's fatal night. I had put more than two dozen teenage burglars in jail, recovered a few thousand dollars worth of stolen property, including two autos, cleared a hundred unsolved break-ins, and now I was left abandoned back at the first hour of the investigation.

"Maybe you're wrong this time, Sasser," David Highbarger suggested. "Maybe it wasn't kids."

"I'm not wrong," I said.

I pondered some more.

"Will you stop talking murders?" Dianne cried in exasperation.

Bill McCracken and I were out with our wives at a night spot.

"There's music and laughter," Dianne said. "Dance with us. There are other things in the world besides people killing each other all the time."

"Not to the victims there isn't," I said.

On June 9 Harley Shaffer telephoned. I had been on him every week to get out and circulate and come up with a name. "The D.A.'s asking me about charges on that Ford you stole," I kept reminding him. With all the snitches I had working the streets, I knew one of them would hit the right combination sooner or later. Kids couldn't do a crime like the Sullivan caper and *not* talk about it.

"Uh, Mr. Sasser," Harley Shaffer began, stumbling, "what I got is, well—I knew some dudes doing a bunch of burglaries. The only one I knew for sure they did is the Porter Mattress Company on Eleventh Street, but there's lots of others. Listen to this, Mr. Sasser. They carry guns. I've seen the guns."

"What are their names?"

"Mike Brown is the only name I know. The other kid's first name is Jimmy. Brown just got out of the Marines. Dishonorably discharged is what I hear."

A make through Records Bureau revealed a Michael

Wayne Brown, eighteen, with a long juvenile rap sheet for burglary and other thefts. It looked promising.

"Mr. Sasser, you gonna take that rap off me now?" Harley Shaffer asked.

I left him dangling. "I'll let you know when, Shaffer."

LZJ proposed we haul Brown in immediately for questioning, but I seldom approached a suspect until I knew at least some of the answers. The answers weren't long in coming. On the morning of June 14, one month to the day after Richard Sullivan fell dead with a bullet in his back, the Homicide phone rang.

"You're asking around about Richard Sullivan," a man's voice began. "I think I can solve it for you. Can you meet me for coffee?"

I even paid for the coffee.

The man in the doughnut shop on Twenty-first Street, around the corner from the murder scene, was short and stocky with a harried middle-aged face. He grabbed a deep, ragged breath before launching into his story about a seventeen-year-old girl named Carla Tanner who was living away from home with a fifteen-year-old boy named Jimmy Joe Horn.

I knew Jimmy Joe. Four years ago, when he was eleven, he was a member of a Boy Scout troop whose boys were being molested by one of the Scout leaders. The leader came to Jimmy Joe's house in the middle of the night pounding on the door and crying for Jimmy Joe to come out. I came out instead and slapped cuffs on the little cocksucker. He broke down and wept and said he was in love with the boy.

Since then I made a habit of personally questioning *anyone* who exerted any control or influence over my sons.

"Carla Tanner," said the man in the doughnut shop, staring into his coffee, "is my daughter."

Carla, he said, had confided in a friend of hers

named Mark Poplin that Jimmy and a boy named Mike were the ones who killed the man in the insurance office.

"Mark can tell you more than I can," the man said.

Mark Poplin could: "Carla told me Jimmy couldn't sleep. She said he lay awake at nights and cried because of what they'd done."

Poplin filled in details.

"Carla said Jimmy stole a gun from Martin's BBQ in a burglary. It was a Colt .22 automatic. Carla, Jimmy, and some guy named Mike broke out a window to get into the insurance building. Some guy came in while they were there, and Mike shot him in the back and killed him. They took the man's wallet and dumped it down a sewer."

I looked at McCracken and hitched up my pants.

"This is it," I said.

It didn't take a Sherlock Holmes to put it together after that. Jimmy Joe lived in a run-down rental off North Sheridan. It was full of cockroaches and mice and greenhead flies. My partner and I caught the kid making his way home on foot across Sheridan. He was a skinny, girlish-looking boy with stringy dark hair hanging down his back. McCracken stomped the accelerator and we bore down on him like Eliot Ness and the Untouchables, going into a skid before I jumped out, threw the skinny kid across the hood, frisked him, handcuffed his hands behind, and flung him into the backseat of the unmarked.

"You're under arrest for first-degree murder, Jimmy Joe!" I barked. "That's the death penalty, boy. *You have the right to remain silent. You have the right to . . .*"

It was all for effect, part of the juvenile interrogation game you had to play with kids because you couldn't question them directly.

"I ain't did nothing, Mr. Sasser," Jimmy Joe screamed.

"Bullshit. You killed a man in cold blood and that's that. We don't want to talk to you about it. William, let's start the kid on that road to the hot seat in Ol' Sparky."

As McCracken took the long, slow way downtown, we kept up a patter of conversation—mostly about where we were going to eat lunch. Jimmy Joe watched, his eyes bulging.

"Mr. Sasser?"

"You know how I feel about killers, Jimmy Joe. Just be quiet."

"Mr. Sasser?"

"I don't want to talk to you, Jimmy Joe."

"I got to tell you something, Mr. Sasser."

"No."

We were stopped for a red light. Jimmy Joe couldn't hold it any longer. I didn't figure he could.

"Mr. Sasser, I ain't killed nobody. Mike did it. Mike Brown killed him!"

The entire story came out in a rush without my asking a single question or violating the boy's civil rights. His body shook so hard from a rush of hot tears that the handcuffs rattled behind his back. I could muster up no sympathy for him.

"I'm the one broke the window," he said through sweat and tears. "But I still didn't kill nobody. I had the gun at first. I was trying to get some money out of a can when I walked into another room and seen that man. I held the man with the gun. Mike came in. So I started shaking. I gave the gun to Mike and I got the guy's wallet. I told Mike not to shoot him. The man said, 'Oh, God, don't shoot. I'll give you all I got.' The gun was only loaded with one bullet. That's all we had—one bullet. I wish we hadn't even had that one.

So I started to leave and Mike told him to turn around. And Mike shot him."

Jimmy Joe wept silently in the backseat.

"Mike's crazy," he cried. "He *liked* the killing!"

Richard Sullivan's wallet had thirty dollars in it. These punks murdered a man for *thirty lousy fucking dollars.*

DON'T MAKE A GOOD KID GO BAD—DON'T BE OUT AT NIGHT WHERE THEY CAN GET TO YOU.

Carla Tanner was next. When she came home to the rental she shared with Jimmy Joe, McCracken and I grabbed her and brought her in for questioning. She was taller than Jimmy Joe and more masculine-looking. She had stringy brown hair and a hooked nose. She looked wrung-out from tension. She said she waited in the car across the street as lookout—cops called it "jiggering"—while the two boys ran behind the insurance building and broke out a window.

"I heard a shot and Mike came out and jumped in the car screaming. He kept on screaming at me, 'Carla, I shot a guy! Carla, I shot a guy!' I backed up the car and Jimmy came running down the road and we let him in. We put the wallet down a drain on Dawson, and then we went back to the apartment. Jimmy started crying and telling me he'd rather have taken a burglary rap than kill somebody.

"I asked him what happened. He said he heard somebody come in, so he pulled the gun and told the guy to give him all his money. He was looking through the wallet, and Mike goes, 'Give me the gun.' Jimmy said he heard Mike telling the guy to turn around. Jimmy closed his eyes and he heard a shot. When he opened his eyes, the guy was on the floor."

Two teenage punks and a stolen gun with one bullet in it. What a combination.

"Mike didn't care at all," Carla went on. "He kept

saying things like, 'I hope he died,' and 'If I'd had another bullet I'd have shot both his eyes out.' Mike told me in the car he couldn't shoot the man to his face, so he made him turn around. I finally told him to shut up."

You couldn't take any chances on a kid like Michael Wayne Brown. He was a hard, cold-blooded killer in spite of his age. Shortly after noon I quietly staked a couple of uniformed officers around Brown's mother's house on the northside, and then McCracken and I went in after him. With guns drawn.

It always annoyed me to hear some joker retiring from a major police department commenting that he never even had to *draw* his gun during twenty years' service, as though that were both something he should be proud of and an indictment of any other cop who did. I figured the reason he never drew his gun was because he was working a school-guard crossing or getting broad in the ass holding down a desk at the station house. Big-city cops working the streets for twenty years, if they're doing a job, are going to at least *draw* their guns.

Brown's mother tried to bar the door; McCracken kicked it open. Then she tried to block the entrance with her body. I flung her against the wall.

"Mike! Run! Run!" the woman screamed down the hallway toward a closed door at the end.

We charged the door, Brown's mother behind us yapping like a terrier. The veins stood out on her forehead like cords. I thought she was going to try to kick me in the nuts.

Mike Brown was still in bed, although it was afternoon. He was a big, strapping kid with short, blond hair. I rammed the muzzle of my big .357 into the soft place in his throat just below his chin. When he opened his eyes, they were a cold gray-blue. He didn't even blink.

"Stealing all night makes you sleep all day, huh?" I growled as I flipped him over in bed and handcuffed him. McCracken kept his mother from getting to me.

"Mike, don't tell these motherfucking pigs nothing till I can get you a lawyer," she ranted.

I thought she was going to kick McCracken in the nuts.

"You slop-sucking pigs is always picking on poor Mike. I better not find a mark on this boy where you pigs beat him neither."

I dragged Brown out of bed. All he wore was his shorts.

"You cocksucker," the woman spat at me.

Brown glared at his mother. "Just shut the fuck up," he told her. And she did.

The kid was hard. He wouldn't say a word about the murder. He just glared at us out of those cold killer's eyes.

"Jimmy is going to testify against you," I said to get him talking.

"You let him tell me that himself."

McCracken escorted Jimmy Joe into the interrogation room. He looked meek, more girlish than ever. McCracken said the wolves at the joint would have him broken over, and be plugging him like a shotgun.

"Would you testify against me, Jimmy Joe?" Brown demanded, his eyes boring holes. "Look me in the eye and tell me you'll testify against me, Jimmy Joe."

Jimmy Joe averted his eyes, shifted his weight. "Mike, you killed that man. I didn't."

Brown glanced away. "Get him out of here," he snarled.

It took a few more days to wrap up the case, recover the murder weapon from a fence Jimmy Joe sold it to afterward, and ferret out a couple of witnesses from

Brown's acquaintances. One of the witnesses was a kid on probation for burglary. He said he saw Mike Brown an hour after the slaying.

"He invited me to go to a restaurant to eat with him. He told me about what had just happened that night. He talked to me about the different things that could have gone wrong. He was mostly concerned about fingerprints. He went over the burglary step by step to see if he had made a mistake somewheres."

Eighteen years old! He executed a man, then went out and had breakfast on the money in the dead man's wallet.

"Sonofabitch," I said. "Sonofabitch."

I removed the last pin from my map and marked Harley Shaffer's auto-theft case exceptionally cleared and closed, no suspects. LZJ came by while I was sitting at my desk staring into the clutter on top of it. He kept grinning and slapping me on the back.

"You did it, Columbo. The chief's pleased."

I looked up. "This really is a fucked-up world. Do you know that, Larry?"

"Make your reports, Sasser," he said.

Jimmy Joe Horn and Carla Tanner turned State's Evidence against Mike Brown. D.A. Buddy Fallis reduced charges against them to accessory to murder. They copped to five years each in the joint, both having been certified to stand trial as adults.

Eventually, the courts commuted Michael Wayne Brown's death penalty to life imprisonment. That's the way it happens most of the time. Five or six years later, Brown was transferred to a minimum-security prison where, among other privileges, convicts received weekend passes and were allowed to go out during the day to work regular jobs. Brown simply walked away. A year later he turned up as the prime suspect in the murders of two New Yorkers who, like Richard Sullivan, apparently surprised him committing a burglary. Brown is still at large.

"What the fuck difference does it make, Columbo?" Doc Roberts asked. His eyes were dark and hard. "We work our asses off trying to protect people from criminals until we can catch them. Then it turns out we can't protect people from the criminals we've already caught. Even if you do collar Mr. Hyde, they'll just fucking let him out again."

The death penalty, if it deters no one else, at least deters the person who receives it.

CHAPTER NINETEEN

"You need a scorecard to tell the freaks apart anymore," Big Bill McCracken murmured in disgust. We were parked in the trees at Mohawk Park, next to the zoo, watching the gays simpering around the rest rooms waiting for someone to give them the eye. The transvestites were out in their hot spring fashions on a warm afternoon—high heels, tight-fitting short skirts, legs shaved, thick makeup concealing their beards. McCracken had just mistaken one of them for a beautiful woman.

"She's going into the men's," I pointed out.

"She's a prostitute," he said hopefully.

"She's a *he.*"

"Oh, God. The zoo's not in *there.*" He pointed across the moat to the lions and tigers and bears and stuff. "The zoo's out *here.*"

The gays had holes drilled through the stall partitions in the men's so they could look at each other and poke their members through the glory holes for their neighbor's pleasure. Gay love apparently didn't mind the ammonia haze of urine or the sounds another neighbor made when he vacated his bowels.

"Partner, I swear we should quit this shitty business," McCracken said. "Living with this shit can't be healthy. It's hazardous to your health."

"You sound like my wife."

"And mine," he replied, grinning.

We weren't in the park just to collect sunshine and observe the wildlife. One of the cruising gays got himself punched permanently on a warm June night the week before. A uniform car came upon the dead man at one A.M. He was slumped over the steering wheel of his Datsun parked underneath an oak tree. He was a huge man—six-two, 270 pounds—but they were soft pounds that made him look more like Huey Duck than an NFL linebacker. The body was clad in white cutoff shorts and a brown T-shirt. Someone had plugged him with a .38 square in the ten ring, right through the heart. Sitting up like that, he hardly bled at all. Blood settled to lividity in his enormous legs and made them purple.

Two things struck me immediately: his underwear lay on the floorboard between his legs, and the wallet left on the passenger's floorboard did not belong to him. It contained identification—no money—belonging to someone named Richard Eugene Harris, who was thirty-two years old, five-ten, 160 pounds, and had black hair. A make on the Datsun's license plate indicated the victim was Paul Shead, twenty-three.

No real whodunit here.

"Put him in jail, Columbo," LZJ said. "That is, if you can drag yourself away from that dead horse you're always beating."

Johnson had about given up on my solving Jekyll and Hyde, but I knew I couldn't. *That* was the case, *my* case, about which Doc Roberts had once commented, "There's at least one that'll come along and get to you." Sometimes I shoved the cardboard box full of case reports to the back of my desk and tried not to even look at it. But then I saw their mutilated bodies in my thoughts—Geraldine's abandoned in the vacant closet, Marie's with the head almost decapitated, Suzanne's in the M.E. office with the maggots in her ear. I *couldn't* let the case go.

In between other homicide investigations I managed to slip a few hours each week to running down new leads. I questioned suspects apprehended for rape and other sex crimes. I took out the case files and pored over them. Had I missed something? I re-questioned possible witnesses.

"Can you remember anything you didn't tell me before?" I demanded.

"Detective Sasser, I'm sorry. This is the fourth time you've asked. I just can't recall anything else."

"Someday I'll have him right here," I kept saying, slowly squeezing my hand into a fist.

LZJ shook his head, slicked down his hair, and walked off. He didn't believe me. Almost two years had passed since Martin. No one believed me anymore.

David Highbarger wanted to know the Big Picture when we carted Paul Shead's oversized corpse to the M.E.'s.

"A queer-bashing?" he asked.

I shook my head. "The angle of the bullet and the range shows the assailant was sitting *inside the car* when he pulled the trigger."

"Maybe it was a robbery," Highbarger proposed. "Wasn't the victim's wallet gone?"

"Shead had taken off his underwear and then put his walking shorts back on," I explained. "The other guy with him—Harris, I presume—lost his wallet on the floorboard when he pulled his pants down around his ankles. It looks like they gave each other blowjobs before the shooting. The killer realized his wallet had fallen out of his pocket. In the dark he felt around and found Shead's wallet lying on the seat. Shead had no pockets in his shorts. In his desperation, the killer thought Shead's wallet was *his* wallet."

Highbarger frowned. "But . . . ?"

"What's the motive?" I grinned thinly.

Cops call gays "butterflies." They flit around like butterflies, getting pollinated as often as they can with as many as they can. They are a volatile bunch, as any cop knows, jealous of each other and always getting into cat fights. Some of them are uncomfortable with their identities, ridden with guilt. They actually hate themselves and they hate others like themselves.

"Are you saying," Highbarger demanded, "that the killer shot Paul Shead because he hates *himself?*"

"What else could it be?" I asked. "He comes to the park, gets what he wants, and then in a fit of guilt he kills the man who gave it to him. I think we'll find Richard Harris to be a married man."

"Did you ever think of going into psychology?" Highbarger asked, impressed.

I ran a make on Harris for his criminal background. I wasn't too surprised to find he was an ex-convict. I was, however, astonished at the nature of his conviction. Sociologists like to say killers make the best risk when it comes to rehabilitation. Yeah. Like the Grinning Hyena. Like Michael Wayne Brown. Like Richard Eugene Harris.

Seven years before in Sequoyah County, Oklahoma, Harris fell for manslaughter. According to the old records, Harris confessed that he and another man believed to be a homosexual were alone in a parked car when they fought over a gun and it discharged, killing the gay. Testimony showed Harris's common-law wife, Lucille, helped him dispose of the death weapon and provided him with an alibi that collapsed under police investigation.

Harris had been granted a governor's release from prison two years ago. The Mohawk Park slaying and the one from Sequoyah County were virtual carbon copies.

"I don't know any Paul Shead," Harris responded immediately after McCracken and I cornered him at a construction site where he worked on the Restless Ribbon.

I sized him up. He had the palest face I had ever seen on a live human, and a paunch that hung over his leather tool belt. His lower lip trembled. Most ex-cons knew the ropes; that made them hard to crack.

"I lost my wallet last night at the Circle Plaza Lounge," he insisted. "I don't have nothing to hide. I don't know how my wallet got in somebody else's car, unless he found it at the bar where I lost it. I've never even been to Mohawk Park."

"Right."

I encouraged him to lay out a story. That way you could go about breaking it down to get to the truth.

He said he worked until four-thirty P.M. the day before. After work he and some hardhats stopped at the Circle Plaza for a few beers. He was completely broke by nine P.M., left the bar alone and went home.

Autopsy showed Shead died around ten P.M.

"It was about nine-thirty when I got home," Harris said. "I told my wife Lucille I had lost my wallet at the bar. We drove around for about ten minutes, then I went home and went to bed. My wallet didn't have any money in it anyhow."

"You didn't bother to go back to the bar where you knew you'd lost it?" I asked casually.

We looked at each other.

"You can ask my witnesses," he said.

"Yeah. Your wife Lucille . . . Didn't she alibi for you the last time too?"

He grew even paler.

Harris had four alibi witnesses this time—his wife, his wife's brother, a cousin by marriage, and the cousin's wife. They said they were all staying in the Harrises' one-bedroom apartment the night of the killing.

"He was home by nine-thirty," the cousin said, and the others backed him up. "I know because me and the ol' lady drove up to the shopping mall on Twenty-first Street to mail a letter. We drove around the shopping center for a while and stopped at Skaggs. Skaggs was closed, so we just window-shopped and then went home. Richard had arrived by that time and was already in bed because he had to work the next day."

Although the odds were a million to one or greater against a man losing his wallet on one end of the city and it ending up an hour later in a murdered man's car, especially if that man had already been convicted of one homosexual killing and the second victim was also a homosexual, I knew I still had to overcome the expected testimony of Harris's four witnesses. Law is rarely based on common sense. This case wasn't so much a *who*dunit as a *prove-it-if-you-can.*

"Richard is always carrying around guns," a hardhat told McCracken and me. He seemed uncomfortable with the role of snitching on a pal. "He had a gun with him in the trunk of his car when we went out drinking beer at the Circle Plaza. It was a new Colt Diamondback revolver. Richard pulled it halfway out of its holster to show me."

"Guns, a phallic symbol," I told David Highbarger. "Macho on the surface to hide his tendencies."

Ballistics analysis of the death bullet indicated it was probably fired by a .38 Colt.

"I like guns," Harris admitted. "I owned a .38 Colt Diamondback, but I couldn't have showed it to nobody. Lucille lost it last weekend. Besides, you know it's against the law for a convicted felon to own a gun."

"Me and my brother was fishing last weekend and I left it on the front of the boat and it fell into Tenkiller Lake," Lucille said.

"How convenient," I cracked.

McCracken thought he had it all figured out.

"Harris came home, all right, just like he said, and he and Lucille went back out," the big cop summarized it. "But it was after midnight. Harris comes running home scared so mama could make everything all right, just like she did in Sequoyah County. They left the apartment to hide the gun and get rid of Paul Shead's wallet. They didn't go back to the bar because Harris *knew* goddamned well *where* he lost his wallet. They might even have gone back to Mohawk Park, but by that time the cops were there."

McCracken frowned. He shifted his weight in the car seat to take the dig of his revolver out of his side.

"Why would a fairly attractive woman make a career out of alibing her freak husband out of fag murders?"

"Let's ask her," I suggested.

We took a search warrant with us. Lucille paced and muttered to herself while my partner and I rummaged through closets and dresser drawers and underneath the bed. We emerged with a recently fired .38 cartridge casing, a .38 S&W in a holster—"That's mine; that's not Richard's," Lucille interjected quickly to protect her husband—and a second empty holster. I tried McCracken's Colt Diamondback in the holster;

it fit like a glove in the worn impression of the previous occupant.

"I don't care what Richard has done," Lucille admitted. "I told you what happened. So did our witnesses."

"There's something badly wrong with your husband," I told her. "This is *twice* he's killed, Lucille. You know it's not going to stop, don't you? Do you want to be responsible for the next one he kills? He's just going to keep at it until we stop him."

For a moment I thought my argument reached her. But then she shook herself.

"Get out of my house!" she suddenly screeched from an anger that seemed more directed at herself than at us. *"Get out! Get out! Goddamn you, I don't want to hear any more!"*

As we drove away, McCracken noted, "Partner, you touched a nerve in there." He looked at me. "There's some fucked-up people in this world," he said.

An attorney telephoned me. "I don't want the police talking to my clients. That includes Richard Harris's family as well as him."

"Don't you think it's odd that people who are supposed to be telling the truth don't want to talk about it?" I asked.

The lawyer sniggered.

I showed the Colt holster to our hardhat witness to see if he could identify it as the one he saw. He looked more uncomfortable than before.

"I don't even know if I saw a gun or not," he stammered.

"What do you mean? You said Richard took it partly out of the holster to show you."

"I just saw the back of the holster and I wasn't paying much attention."

"You're telling me Richard brought you out to his car trunk to show you the back of a holster?"

The hardhat's eyes wouldn't meet mine.

"You're lying through your teeth," I said bluntly.

He swallowed. He looked constipated.

"We don't think Richard killed that queer," the hardhat murmured.

"Then stick with the facts and let the facts prove it one way or another. Don't lie for the man."

"Richard ain't no queer."

So that was it? If Harris killed Shead in Mohawk Park, it meant he was probably gay. These big macho hardhats couldn't admit they might be buddies with a homosexual.

The hardhat scuffed his boot. He dragged off his tin hat and wiped away sweat. He gazed off into the sun.

"Richard ain't no queer," he repeated.

You couldn't fret over a setback.

Inside Harris's wallet found in Shead's Datsun was a sales slip folded into a tiny square. It was a receipt from a Radio Shack located only a few blocks from Paul Shead's residence. It was made out to "Paul Shee," but it correctly listed Shead's address. It was dated a week before he died.

Although a lawyer might successfully argue that the deceased put it in the wallet after he found it and before he was murdered, common sense told you there was more to it than that. It meant the suspect and victim knew each other *before* the fatal night. When the clerks at the store could not remember the "Paul Shee" customer, it sent McCracken and me to cruising Mohawk Park in search of a witness who might have seen the two men together, either that last night or before.

Mostly, gays didn't like to talk to the police, but you

could get to them if you knew how. Some of the cruisers were married men, professionals like doctors and lawyers who had this one little quirk—they liked to suck dicks, as McCracken put it. They were also willing to flap their jaws more than in the rest rooms if you caught them going down on somebody and just happened to mention how devastating it would be to their careers if they were busted for sodomy.

We surprised a postal worker like that who admitted he knew Paul Shead in the biblical sense. He said he saw Shead in the park at nine-fifteen the night of the murder.

"He looked like he was waiting for somebody."

A black kid in tight short shorts, so sweet he looked like he was trying to fly, smacked his lips and fluttered his wrist. He batted his eyes. "I just adore big, strong, macho *policemen,*" he cooed.

McCracken rolled his eyes.

"Light your sweet ass here for a minute," McCracken said. "We want to ask you some questions."

"I met Richard Harris in Mohawk Park eight months ago," Tinker Bell said. "I had *wonderful* sex with him *three* times." He held up three fingers for emphasis, fluttered his wrist coyly, then frowned. "Then he started acting kind of weird."

"Weird?"

"Yes. Dear, dear me. He called me a 'cocksucker' and said he hated me. It was such a shame. Paul and I used to talk about Mr. Harris—what he looked like, the type of car he drove . . ."

"Then Paul Shead and Richard Harris knew each other?"

"Oh, yes. Paul said Richard really had a swell body."

"He's pot-gutted."

"You foolish boy. That's *not* what you look at."

"Did you happen to see the two of them together at any time?"

"No . . ."

The patrolman who discovered Shead dead at one A.M. noted that the Datsun's headlights and ignition were on but the battery and engine were as dead as the driver. I experimented to see how long it took a car battery like Shead's to die if the engine quit with the headlights on. It took approximately three hours. That meant the Datsun had sat in the park with the lights on since about nine-thirty or ten.

The gay postal worker saw Shead at nine-fifteen P.M. waiting for someone. The autopsy gave Shead's time of death as about ten P.M. Harris left the Circle Plaza bar at nine P.M. It was 15.7 miles from the bar to Mohawk Park, a driving time of thirty-five minutes if you obeyed speed limits. Harris could have met Shead in the park around 9:35, accomplished his sordid business, and then arrived home around ten-thirty or eleven while Paul Shead's body cooled out in the park.

Everything was circumstantial; I started adding up the circumstances:

Harris claimed he "lost" his wallet at nine P.M., only to have it surface 15.7 miles away an hour later in a dead man's car.

Paul Shead's sales slip was in Richard Harris's wallet.

Harris claimed his wife "lost" a .38 Colt revolver, which just happened to be the right type of murder weapon, only a week before the murder.

On the search warrant against Harris's apartment, McCracken and I recovered a .38 cartridge casing—*souvenir?*—and a holster broken in for a .38 Colt.

Rather than commit perjury when it came

down to it, the hardhat would likely testify he saw Harris with a Colt revolver a few hours before the slaying.

Other gays had seen Harris cruising in Mohawk Park, countering Harris's claims that he was not homosexual and had never been to Mohawk Park; one even claimed to have had sex with him.

From witnesses and the sales slip in Harris's wallet, we could certainly infer that Harris and Shead were acquainted before their last rendezvous.

Circumstantial, but impressively circumstantial. It was as good as the Robert Asberry case, in which Asberry knocked off his sister-in-law Brenda Nelson in a rape killing. The victim was the sister of a Tulsa patrolman. Her body ended up in a field, burned, and her bones scattered by coyotes and skunks. Asberry, an ex-con for rape, wouldn't talk about it.

"I ain't going back to the joint again." That was all he said.

"It'll never fly," LZJ said, shaking his head.

"It's intricate, it's complicated," I agreed. "But if we can make a jury go through it step by step—there's only one conclusion."

D.A. Buddy Fallis studied the case and studied it. "We'll never get a conviction," he concluded, "but damnit, the sonofabitch is guilty and we ought to make a run at him anyhow."

Sometimes juries understand circumstances better than hard evidence. It took a district court jury only two hours of deliberations before it slam-dunked Asberry for second-degree murder.

"But Asberry didn't have four alibi witnesses like Harris does," the D.A. said.

The Shead investigation went on stalemate. It stayed like that month after month. It was frustrating, having a killer walking around free, gloating over his "perfect crime," but it was still nothing like the pressures involved in the Jekyll-and-Hyde thing. I *knew* who Paul Shead's killer was; it was still just a matter of proving it.

"Don't get cocky on me," I warned Harris. "The next time you see me coming—I'm coming for you."

It would be a while, though, before that happened.

LZJ slicked down his hair. "Columbo, you're slipping. How many unsolved cases do you have in that desk drawer trash bin of yours? Martin, Rosenbaum, Oakley, that ten-year-old kid found in the woods, and now Shead."

It didn't do any good to argue that *no* detective solved *every* case.

"The Gray Ghost is on my ass," LZJ said. "Put somebody in jail."

CHAPTER TWENTY

At some point during each year near the anniversary of the death of one of the three girls, Jack Wimer of the Tulsa *Tribune* published a feature update about the homicides. During the second year, he wrote:

> Chuck Sasser, Tulsa homicide detective, has been assigned to solve the Martin-Rosenbaum-Oakley cases. He has interviewed more than 1500 persons, and jailed briefly 30 persons for questioning. Investigator Sasser receives calls about the cases each day.
>
> He takes names. He interviews people. He pores over notes scribbled on the backs of envelopes six or eight months ago. He spends most of his time interviewing people with strange quirks or bizarre sexual habits.
>
> Wednesday, Sasser received some information about a man in a bar talking about Ms. Martin's death. Today, he will try to find that man. When Sasser left the office today he had no idea if that man would indeed be the psychopathic killer or

just another of the 1500 persons he has interviewed in these cases.

In any event, this day for police will be much like the last 365, demanding hard work, and holding out that elusive hope of success.

Of course, there were other girl murders, some of them just as bizarre as the Jekyll-and-Hyde case. One girl had her throat slit and was dropped off a bridge into a creek. Another was found staked out nude in a north Tulsa County pasture with a persimmon limb rammed up her vagina. But it seemed the Jekyll-and-Hyde murders were the ones that caught and held the public's imagination, as they had caught and held me for the nearly three years since I pulled the sheet off Suzanne Oakley's corpse at the M.E. morgue.

It haunted me that this psychopath who raped and mutilated young women was still lurking somewhere out there because I wasn't smart enough or lucky enough to catch him. Sometimes the thought entered my mind that he might have left Tulsa, slithering off to another city to carry out his foul deeds, but I refused to believe it. He was still here. I could feel him. He walked out there somewhere, he talked, he laughed, he prowled the streets, he watched TV, he *lived* while his victims were dead.

All I had to do was find him. Or *them*.

It drove me.

One after the other I tracked down suspects in every violent sex crime reported to police. I collared voyeurs, rapists, first-degree burglars who stole and ate women's panties. A freak I was questioning suddenly produced a knife and lunged at me with it. I had been stabbed once before, years ago, in the back by a pimp, but this time I saw it coming. I should have killed the man, but I didn't. First, I had to make sure he wasn't

Mr. Hyde. I sidestepped his thrust and knocked him flat on his face on the floor with an ax-hand chop to the back of the neck. I took the knife from him and held him on the floor. I heard the small bones in his wrist cracking from the pressure of my holding him there, but I broke his wrist anyhow and kept him on the floor while he babbled in response to my questions.

When I was certain he was not my man, I stood up, kicked him hard in the guts for trying to stab me, and walked out.

"Fuck him," I muttered. "I really should have killed the scumbag. He doesn't deserve to live."

Still another freak exploded into a rage when he found out what I wanted. He tore his house apart. He made kindling of tables and chairs. He hurled lamps through his windows. I leaned against the wall out of his way, hitched up my trousers, and waited until he was exhausted. Then I finished questioning him.

"You're right, Doc," I said to Roberts. "The world has terminal weirdness. There are no *normal* people."

"Bingo!" McCracken kept saying. "Bingo!"

"He's out there laughing at me," I said.

I picked word off the streets that a man named Melvin Cauley was talking around that he was the one who killed Geraldine Martin. The man had real possibilities.

"He's a space jockey," Doc Roberts commented. "Maybe he *is* your Okie Chokie."

I took to his trail. It was going to be hard to run him down and surprise him. My presence in the city made Melvin's life a little hell. He was always keeping an eye peeled for me. Just walking down the street, he kept his head swiveling back and forth, and his nose that had been broken a few times and was all scarred and smashed flat to his face would be sniffing the city fumes. His wild eyes with all the white in them flitted constantly. He took off running anytime he spotted me. Sometimes if I happened to see him first I goosed my car and bore down on him just to see him jump and run.

Once, he was looking back over his shoulder at me and running when he ran into a wall and knocked himself cold. I stuffed one of my police business cards into his shirt pocket. He told a counselor at the Tulsa Psychiatric Center that I tried to kill him.

"Sasser's gonna do me, man," he whined in desperation. "Can't you see what he is? Did you look at his eyes? Sasser might be a cop, but he's a hit man too. He's gonna kill me."

I laughed. "Not yet," I said.

The "hit man" thing started a few years earlier when one of my street snitches—a squirrel who bragged around that he worked for the FBI—passed on information that Cauley, who was out on an armed-robbery bail bond, wanted to hire someone to knock off the prosecution witness. My snitch set up Cauley for a meeting with a "professional hit man."

I slipped on dark glasses and a red sport shirt and became a caricature of a bad man. I climbed a dingy stairway to an even dingier room where Melvin waited. He was big and rawboned, with scars and some teeth missing—typical street thug. He looked mean enough to take on a wolverine. I stepped right into him, forcing him back a step. I didn't say anything for a long moment. I just stood there looking at him through dark glasses. I had my shirt hiked up just a little so he would be sure to glimpse the big .357 stuck in my belt.

Melvin's eyes kept shifting from his reflection in my glasses to the nickel glint of the gun at my waist. He started trembling.

At long last I said, "You wanted me?"

"Oh. Yeah. Okay."

He couldn't take his eyes off the gun.

"Are you tryin' to waste my fuckin' time?" I snapped.

"No, sir. I wouldn't do that, sir."

"Then spell it out, mister. What do you want? I got a cunt waitin' for me. I don't need you fuckin' with me too."

He had to be the one to initiate the conspiracy. Otherwise, the courts called it entrapment.

"No, sir. I mean, yes, sir. I wouldn't waste your time, sir."

He lapsed nervously into how he had gone barefaced into a liquor store to rob it. The liquor-store owner was the only witness.

"I wouldn't be going back to the joint if he disappeared," Cauley proposed.

I patted my gun butt. "You want me to . . . ? Is that right?"

It took Cauley three or four attempts before he could swallow. Then his voice sounded like it was being held between two bricks.

"I'll give you five hundred dollars and a GTO with a getaway engine in it."

"Shee-*it.*"

"Shit?"

"I want a thousand. Five hundred now and five hundred when I finish the job. I want it in small bills. I'll let you know where I want it delivered. Forget the GTO with the getaway engine."

Cauley fidgeted.

I said, "I had better get all my money too."

Beads of sweat popped out on his face like blisters.

"You'd be the last man I cheated," he stammered. "I could tell you was a hit man when I seen you."

"I'd do you for free if you cheated me."

"Man, I wouldn't *never* do that."

When the scam went down and Cauley ended up back in jail, he refused to believe I was anything other than a hit man. Melvin was so jumpy about me now that he had been paroled again and I wanted to question him about Geraldine Martin, that he slipped out of my grasp three or four times before patrolmen managed to corner him in a shooting gallery frequented by hepatitis hypes. I went upstairs to the jail to bring him down to the interrogation cubicle in the bullpen. He grabbed the bars so hard his knuckles turned white.

"Don't make me go with him!" he howled. "Help me. Please? He's gonna kill me."

McCracken had to bring him down.

"Don't lie to me, Melvin," I warned after we had him trapped in one of the cubicles.

"I'd *never* lie to you, Mr. Sasser, sir."

McCracken grinned. I Mirandaized the ex-convict and got down to business. Cauley opened up immediately.

"I been dreaming about Geraldine," he volunteered.

I looked at him. A man who couldn't face his guilt directly often "dreamt" a confession. I saw McCracken edge up on his chair toward the suspect. I cast him a quick warning glance: *Don't get too eager and make him clam up.*

"Tell me about it, Melvin," I encouraged, sounding as though we might be discussing the weather or a new movie.

"I see these two figures," Cauley narrated. "One of them is Geraldine Martin and the other is a man, but I never see the man's face when I dream it. It's like he's always in the dark, but she's where I can see her.

Geraldine and whoever the man is are connected by a love line. He loves Geraldine. I can see them behind the apartments. It's dark and there's a struggle."

His breathing had increased until he was panting. He suddenly jumped to his feet, eyes bulging.

"Take me to the Osage Shopping Center!" he shouted. "I'll show you where I see them in my dreams."

We worked north out of downtown and passed the Osage Center, located across the street from the abandoned apartments in which we had found Geraldine's body three winters ago. McCracken drove while I concentrated on Cauley riding handcuffed and silent in the backseat of the unmarked Torino. I noted that Cauley didn't even glance toward the murder scene.

McCracken drove slowly. Cauley peered around. Two blocks past the Osage Apartments he nodded at an apartment complex.

"Behind there," he directed.

"Are you sure—" McCracken started, but I caught his eye.

The Torino crept into the alleyway behind the building. I watched Cauley intensely study his surroundings. Even a space cadet like Cauley would remember where the crime occurred—if he were the one who committed it. We were two blocks away from it. I said nothing. I waited.

"Stop!"

Cauley's scream of anguish sent ice up my spine. McCracken braked. The car engine idled. I watched in astonishment as the big man in the backseat collapsed into a formless pile of heart-rending sobs.

"This is it!" he cried. "This is where it happened. He's killing her! Oh, my God! My God! I can see his face. It's me! It's *me!"*

* * *

"That's a *confession,*" LZJ said, stunned when I signed Melvin Cauley's release from jail.

"He didn't do it either," I replied wearily. Cauley had none of his facts right.

LZJ shook his head and walked off. I slumped at my desk to brood. I dragged out all the old Jekyll-and-Hyde files. I pored over them. I couldn't let it go. Everytime I dragged in another prisoner, some of them scratching and biting and spitting, LZJ slicked down his hair and asked, "Is this the one?" But it never was.

Dianne watched me, and I saw the unhappiness in her growing. McCracken watched me too.

"Partner, you have to know when to let go," he said.

I couldn't let go, not until Mr. Hyde paid for his crimes.

"I'll catch him," I promised.

Jack Wimer, the reporter, caught me at my desk late one evening. He was out trying to dig up a headline.

"Chief Purdie finally making you clean up your desk?" he asked smugly.

I looked up. "Maybe you'll have a different story to write next anniversary," I said.

I returned to my files. Maybe I had neglected something simple and vital along the way that would lead me to the killer.

But if I had, I couldn't find it.

CHAPTER TWENTY-ONE

Fourteen months had elapsed since Paul Shead got himself killed in what I called the Mohawk Park Murder. I had investigated other homicides since then, and I had continued to run through an apparently endless stream of Jekyll and Hydes. One afternoon McCracken and I were following a lead on an armed-robbery shooting. It was August, approaching the third anniversary of Suzanne Oakley's death. I pulled in front of the Skaggs Store on Twenty-first Street and stopped so McCracken could dash in for a pack of cigarettes. I waited with the engine running and air-conditioning going, thinking about our latest case and the best way to nab the killer.

McCracken came hurrying back into the sunlight wearing a grin that stretched the scar on his lip halfway across his face.

I looked at him. "Heat stroke," I guessed.

He ignored the remark. "What time did Richard Harris's cousin say he and his wife came to Skaggs that night to mail their letter?" he asked.

He knew Harris's alibi as well as I.

"Humor me," he requested, still grinning.

"Senility," I decided, but I accommodated him anyhow, saying, "It was nine-thirty P.M. They said they were here just a few minutes. When they went back to the apartment, Richard had come home and was already in bed."

McCracken wouldn't stop his foolish grinning.

"What did they say about Skaggs?" he asked.

"They said Skaggs was closed."

McCracken gave a whoop and slammed his palm against the car dash.

"We got that little cocksucker now!" he shouted.

I didn't get it.

"Look at the sign in the window," McCracken directed triumphantly. "Skaggs closes at *midnight.* I checked while I was in there. It also closed at midnight on the night Harris killed Paul Shead."

Stunned, I slipped forward until my forehead pressed against the steering wheel. For fourteen months I had overlooked something simple that would destroy Richard Harris's alibi. I couldn't help thinking with a sinking feeling that if I had been so clumsy in the Mohawk Park case, might I not have been equally clumsy in the Jekyll-and-Hyde whodunit?

"I should have caught that," I murmured.

McCracken sobered. "Partner," he said, "not even Columbo can think of everything."

"But don't you see? A killer may be getting away with three murders because I've overlooked something."

Richard Harris almost fainted when he looked up from working at a West Tulsa construction site and spotted me striding toward him. He straightened up and stared. Even from a distance I could see him start to tremble.

"Run, you maggot," I whispered fiercely to myself. "Give me an excuse to blast your ass."

He stood there between two piles of lumber, staring. The bloodred morning sun that a homicide cop would always notice rosed out his pale face. He worked outdoors, but he never seemed to tan.

I walked up to him.

"I've come for you, Richard," I said. "I told you a year ago I would. You're under arrest for murder. 'You have the right to remain silent. Anything you say can and will be used against you in a court of law. You have the right . . .' "

"Columbo always gets his man!" LZJ cheered.

Not always.

None of Harris's alibi witnesses dared testify for him at his trial. The D.A. was prepared to charge them with perjury. Harris drew a sentence of ten-to-life for second-degree murder. I drew a four-pointed Star of David on my desk pad. On each of three points I scribbled one of their names—*Geraldine, Marie, Suzanne.* On the fourth point I wrote: *Attention to detail.*

CHAPTER TWENTY-TWO

It was spring again. Showers splashed a gray sheet of water against the long narrow windows that looked out of the detectives bullpen onto Fifth Street. A black man wearing soiled green work clothing wandered into the bullpen. He stopped at the door and glanced around. Four or five detectives were at their desks in Burglary and Forgery. Curt Hanks's desk was nearest the door. He glanced up from his paperwork.

The black man said, "Some officers told me to see Detective Columbo."

"Over there," Hanks said, gesturing.

The visitor stopped at my desk. "I want to see Detective Columbo."

"That's what they call me."

"My name be Willie Smith."

I looked him over. He was about thirty, with nappy hair clotted with lint, and he had body odor and bad breath. I figured him for a street person hanging around downtown begging quarters to buy Night Train Express.

"We done it," Willie Smith announced, staring without blinking.

I pushed my chair back. "Done what?"

"We-all kilt that white girl in the park. Me an' Robber Jones an' Danny Lewis."

I scrutinized him carefully, probing his unblinking eyes. You never knew. I recited him his Miranda warning.

"Now you can tell me about it."

He did.

"We seen her in the park, see, an' we yanked her off the trail. We done it, see, 'cause we wanted us some money an' we wanted us some pussy. Mostly, we wanted us some pussy. We robbed her first an' then we tricked her into askin' us to kill her. We tol' her we *wouldn't* kill her if she tol' us to do it, but if she tol' us *not* to, we *would.* So she tol' us to do it, see, so we done it. That's how we tricked her."

Workmen making River Park safe had cleared out all the underbrush except for the thicket that marked that now-long-ago crime scene. I kept asking that it be left. A dead tree leaned across the pathway that entered the tiny glade where Reverend Arthur Manis found Suzanne Oakley's body. The trail was the only way into the little clearing through near-impenetrable brush. The real killer would know that.

I drove Willie Smith to the park and stopped near the dead tree.

"Show me where you did it," I instructed him.

Willie blinked for about the first time, looking. Finally, he pointed to the thick clump of trees. "Ain't that it right there?"

"Go down there and show me where you left the body."

Reluctantly, Willie Smith clambered out of the car and stood foolishly in the rain. I stayed inside the car. My windshield wipers cut broad swaths across the glass.

"Go on," I said. "Show me."

Willie took a few tentative steps toward the bushes. He hesitated and looked back. I motioned for him to go on. He ventured down the little grassy knoll from the jogging trail, stared at the brambles and knitted willows and maples, then plunged headlong into the thicket. His struggle to get through made bushes shake and trees vibrate. He hadn't even looked for the pathway in.

"Cocksucker," I muttered, and drove off, leaving Willie Smith alone to fight his own way in and out. Where did all the creeps keep coming from?

"I'm a paranoid schizophrenic," Nick Piltz self-diagnosed. He possessed a narrow, sensitive face with flaring pink nostrils and thin pale hands. He said he was an artist.

He proudly showed me some of his paintings—Dracula with blood-dripping fangs; Satan in schizophrenic electriclike strokes; girls crawling out of caskets with their heads tucked underneath their arms and captions below that read, "Take off your head and stay awhile."

Piltz was a nonstop talker, hyperactive.

"I'm homosexual, but I don't kill girls," he said at the beginning of a monologue that plunged into forbidden recesses of a tormented mind. "I'm trying to give up being homosexual. I've progressed to bisexuality. I'm interested in women, but I'm still interested in men too. I have a friend, Jack Burris, who goes around bragging about rectal intercourse. I'd never do that. It doesn't hurt to do it with my mouth, but my ass is for sitting and shitting and that's it.

"Jack doesn't have any real family, so he finds strangers to live with him. He likes girls too, but he can't get any because of his poor personality. He blames his father for his homosexuality. I blame my mother for the way I turned out. Sometimes I think I should kill her. Maybe I will. She's very dominant. She used to kick me. She's a counselor for the welfare department. It's good therapy for her.

"I told those lies about killing two people and burying them because I wanted to sound vicious so I could join the Hell's Angels. The only thing I know about that girl from Tulsa Junior College is they found her stuffed in a closet. I was really upset when the jogger was killed. I tried to organize some vigilantes to go to River Park and stake it out to find the killer. I couldn't get anybody interested—apathy, you know—so after a while I lost interest too.

"I haven't heard any more about them because I don't read the newspapers and don't watch television. All that violence in the media drives me crazy."

It seemed everyone in the world had his little kinks and dark secrets. And there I was, trudging from town houses to rat-infested housing projects, from exclusive social clubs to whorehouses, from lawyers' offices to psycho wards, the capitol building to a skid-row flophouse, trying to ferret out the dark secret of who killed, mutilated, and raped my three girls. I looked in the mirror at a face that seemed to be growing harder and older, but I shrugged it off and kept going. You couldn't walk through a sewer, cops said, and not get shit on you. But I had my second skin, and none of it touched me.

"Chuck, I need a rainbow," Officer Monte Peterson would say, and we would go out for pizza or something and I would let her talk it out.

What happens someday if *I* need a rainbow? I wondered once, but I shrugged that off too. I kept hearing Officer McFann's voice from the Miami Police Academy.

"I am going to make a man out of you," he said. "A police*man*. A police*man* is tough. The shit can't get to a police*man*. A police*man* is at war! In the streets you are *The Man!*"

Mama Pat, who called herself the "Go-Go Grandma" in the skid-row bars, also ran a two-bit cathouse on North Main in a condemned building. There was no running water upstairs, so the girls used a common bucket of water to douche themselves after a trick. Mama Pat was always at her window keeping a watch for the Vice Squad. When she spotted me pull to the curb, her laughing voice boomed across the street. Her roaring foul tongue reminded me of Grace at The Fowler House.

"Chuckie!" Grace called me that too. "Chuckie, you fuckin' little porker. Did you come to fuck or talk?"

"Mama Pat, you know you're the only broad got my eye," I teased. "But you've retired from the cribs."

"One of these days," she promised, "I'm gonna make you fish or cut bait."

A good detective cultivates hookers and numbers runners and bar girls and other petty hustlers. People in Vice know what's happened in a city, from its highest level to its lowest.

"It wouldn't surprise me one cunt's hair if these two motherfuckers I know didn't kill your three girls," Mama Pat said after she pounded on a Coke machine in the lobby to knock loose a couple of cans, kicked some empty wine bottles from in front of her door, and showed me to her sofa that had lost two legs on one end and was propped up on cans of Coke.

She told me how two of her girls were meeting a Tulsa politician and his friend, a wealthy hotel owner, every Friday night in a reserved suite of rooms. The two men were heavy into S&M—sadomasochism. They snapped big safety pins through the heads of their penises and took on the prostitutes and each other like that. They jabbed fish hooks through their scrotums and tied line to them, at the ends of which they attached bowling balls for them to drag. They paid the call girls to urinate in their faces and they ate feces. Mama Pat said the pair finally got so kinky none of the girls wanted to go there anymore, no matter how good the money.

"Cocksuckers like that," Mama Pat concluded, "are probably killers too."

McCracken and I went out after the shift for drinks. Sometimes you needed a drink.

I said, "Goddamn, William, nothing is ever what it seems to be or should be. State senators are out molesting six-year-old girls, preachers are fucking the deacon's wife, and the priest is diddling the choir boy. You look at little churchgoing Mollie in the neighborhood and you think she's all so prim and proper and wholesome and *good.* Turns out she's screwing the neighbor's dachshund while he takes pictures of it to sell to a policeman. Seeing this shit all the time makes you wonder about your own wife. Hell, it makes you wonder about *yourself.* Isn't there anything *good* left in the world?"

McCracken didn't say anything for a few minutes. He studied his glass, drank, and ordered another round.

"There's nothing that you or anyone else can do that will ever make a difference," he said.

I looked at him.

"It's a fucked-up society," he said. "Liberal judges and lawyers and politicians have turned everything upside down. Just accept it and forget it. It don't mean nothing. You can't change it, Columbo. Nobody can."

I kept staring.

"William, we have got to make a difference," I said. "We have got to believe we can."

"No," he replied. "You can't change it; it changes *you*—or it kills you."

Threatening phone calls from a man who said he was the Jekyll-and-Hyde killer sent frightened women scurrying in droves to my desk in the bullpen.

"Don't hang up on me or I'll kill you," the caller typically said. "Did you read about the girl who was raped and killed on the Arkansas River? Well, I did it. Do you want to know how I did it? First, I raped her. Second, I cut off her breasts. Then I put her in the river."

I went after him. He might be deliberately distorting the facts. One day, one of these kooks would be the *right* kook.

The calling continued for nearly three months, over six hundred calls apparently at random from the telephone book, before the freak got hung up on one of his victims. Her name was Terri. She had a throaty voice that exuded sex. The man started calling her four or five times a week. I asked Terri to keep him interested, help me trap him.

"Terri, it's me. John Clark."

He had used about a dozen different aliases.

"Hi, John," Terri replied. We had worked out a signal so she could contact me quickly on a separate phone.

"Do you still think you killed a girl, John?" Terri asked.

"Yes, but I won't kill you, Terri. I like you."

"I think I might like you, John, if I could get to know you."

"You'd tell the police."

"John, would I do that to someone I liked?"

"I don't know. Terri, do you know what I'm doing right now?"

"What are you doing, John? Something fun?"

"I'm beating my meat while I'm talking to you on the phone."

"How darling. Wouldn't you like me to do it for you?"

"Yes. Yes. But I don't trust you."

He hung up each time before the phone company could get a trace.

"Next time," I reassured Terri. He was weakening; I knew he couldn't resist much longer.

"I'm frightened," Terri said. "What if he tries to come to my house?"

"If I'm not watching you, some other policeman is. We won't let him near you."

The next time the scumbag called, he said, "I trust you, Terri. Promise me you won't call the police?"

"Promise him anything," I instructed. "It doesn't mean anything."

Terri succeeded in setting up a rendezvous on Utica Avenue. I slipped on an old pair of jeans, sneakers, and a ratty shirt, and started patrolling Utica on foot. When a rattletrap Dodge passed twice, occupied by a single white male, I faded into an alley where I could watch the rendezvous site. The Dodge parked down the block and the driver got out. I knew it was John Clark from the phone description he gave Terri—long, stringy hair, a wispy black beard, stocky, wrapped in a mackinaw coat, about twenty-five years old.

He trotted across Utica with his hands thrust deep in his baggy jeans, his head ratcheting back and forth suspiciously. He waited on the corner for Terri. He seemed wired.

I started casually down the sidewalk toward him, pretending interest in the autos on a used-car lot. Terri wasn't going to meet John Clark; *I* was, as soon as I was near enough to reach him with the long arm of the law.

I don't know how, but he made me. Maybe he recognized me from my pictures in the paper, since he seemed to have followed the Jekyll-and-Hyde investigation in the news. Maybe it was just that instinct creeps have for spotting cops.

His busy eyes locked onto me. Then he bolted.

"Oh, shit!" I muttered, and the race was on.

I was a runner. I ran two or three miles every day to keep in shape. I once chased down a twenty-year-old basketball player, ran him for over a mile up Utica to Pine Street. He kept looking back over his shoulder and his eyes got huge as I gained on him. I finally got close enough to boot him in the ass with a flying field-goal kick that sent him sliding out of bounds on his face.

If I could do that, I knew John Clark didn't stand a chance. He raced down a block, cut across a yard, and took an alley. I was right behind him. I did a quick little field-goalie's hop, like I had with the basketball player, and punted John Clark across a row of garbage cans. Before he had a chance to recover, I was astraddle him and giving him a chance to look down the long, dark barrel of my .357 magnum. It was the era of the Clint Eastwood *Dirty Harry* movies. "Make my day," Dirty Harry said before he blew away some crud.

"Make my day," I said.

He didn't make my day.

The creep's real name was Joe Snyder. He talked until he was hoarse. He grabbed the edges of his chair in the interrogation room and begged.

"I didn't kill nobody. Honest. I can't help doing what I do. Something comes over me everytime I see a telephone. Don't you see? All my life I've been a nobody. I thought if I frightened girls, they wouldn't hang up on me. Even if I got caught, it was nothing. It was nothing, but it was still *something.* Don't you understand? I didn't kill any girls, but I thought if you arrested me for murder, people would respect me because they thought I killed somebody."

"Terminal weirdness," I said to Doc Roberts.

Snyder's entire family was, as Doc put it, a few loads shy of a brickyard. His brother Harold giggled and played with his balls when you tried to talk to him. Two-hundred-pound sister Carol took turns bedding with brother Harold and two uncles.

"Harold said he loves me. He wants to marry me and us live together."

"It's against the law for a brother and sister to marry."

"We found that out when we went to get the marriage license. Then we was just going to live together."

None of this perturbed the matriarch of the clan.

"I suppose it's a natural thing," she said matter-of-factly, "what with Carol's age and her not being good-looking and all. Besides, it don't hurt nothing."

I stared at her.

"Your son hasn't killed anyone," I finally told her in exasperation. "I'm charging him with misdemeanors for making obscene telephone calls. But I'll break his fucking fingers if I catch his grubby little fist wrapped around another telephone."

Fat Mama Snyder clambered to her feet. She was red-faced. "Our attorney will hear how you talked to us," she promised.

I flipped my business card on the floor and walked out.

Harold Snyder died a year later of a heroin overdose, Carol moved in with an uncle. Every so often Joe Snyder made just one more telephone call.

"I just can't resist. I'm a nobody."

"Put somebody in jail," LZJ kept saying.

CHAPTER TWENTY-THREE

In Homicide, as Doc Roberts liked to say, we had job security. There was always someone killing someone else. Sometimes I thought it bitterly funny that so much of my living was occupied with dying. Death became kind of a cruel joke, some of the shit that your cop's skin shed for you. You laughed in its face; a person's violent death became nothing more than a puzzle to be solved. At least most of the time it did.

On a March morning when icy fingers still reached down skid-row sewers, Doc Roberts and I met M.E. Investigator Dave Highbarger, a Burglary dick called J.L.R. "Bullets" Brown, and a uniformed cop in the dingy lobby of the downtown Cotton Hotel.

"It looks like a suicide," said Bullets Brown. "He strangled himself to death. I've seen 'em do it like that before. Everyone in the hotel says he's an alkie and was despondent."

Bullets led the way along a dim tunnel that smelled of mold to a second-floor room where a bony old man lay sprawled dead on his back across a bed. Doc and I stood silently in the doorway, taking in the room and its deceased occupant.

The room measured about eleven by sixteen, with a single window above a steam radiator looking out into a narrow dead-end alley one floor below. It hadn't been cleaned since about 1960. Trash and empty wine bottles littered the floor and windowsill. The only furnishings consisted of the bed, a battered dresser, a night table, and an open closet. I wrinkled my nose at the odor.

The dead man's feet dangled off the side of the bed. He was still wearing his shoes, along with dark brown trousers and a long-sleeved shirt. His face above a neck around which a pillowcase was knotted tightly was puffed out and blue-mottled and as gross as a hunk of rotted beef. The old man's claws clutched at the knot of the pillowcase.

I checked rigor mortis by lifting an elbow. As stiff as a dead fish. I noted the time: eight A.M. He probably died sometime around or shortly before eight yesterday evening.

The manager's name was Maggie May Catch. I thought she was a man when I first saw her. She wore a crew cut and an old-fashioned man's business suit set off by a wide bright yellow tie mottled by food stains. She said the dead man, Theodore Duke, had lived in the hotel one month. He came in yesterday afternoon to pay his rent for another month. He was so drunk he fumbled with his wallet for some minutes before he was able to extract two twenties and a ten. Maggie said he had fourteen dollars left in his wallet after he paid his rent.

I left the door to the room open because I wanted to look over the other hotel residents who gathered in the hallway to watch. They were a seedy bunch. One man in a wheelchair was complaining because everyone got in front of him and he couldn't see.

"Who discovered the body?" I asked Maggie May Catch.

She pointed to a short, stocky man younger than the others. He looked about forty. He wore a beige see-through nylon shirt with a can of Prince Albert tobacco in his breast pocket.

"Bill Houck," Maggie May said. "He's the maintenance man."

Doc and I extracted a few more facts—Houck discovered the old man dead at about seven-thirty A.M.; no, there were no strangers in the hotel, and no one had been hanging around—before I nodded at Roberts.

"You want to tell them, Doc?"

The detective turned his amused eyes on the gathering.

"This is no suicide," he announced. "What we have here is a case of homicide."

Bill Houck's eyes bulged. *"Murder?"*

Doc looked at him. "As sure as Doan's makes little liver pills," he said.

"Why in Heaven's name would somebody murder an old drunk like Mr. Duke?" Maggie May asked.

I pointed to how the victim's trousers were twisted around to reveal a gaping left rear pocket. The pocket was empty. "For the fourteen dollars in his wallet," I said. "Life comes cheap."

The maintenance man stepped forward. "Maybe whoever did it left his wallet in the hotel somewhere," he suggested. "I'll go look in all the trash cans."

He scurried off.

Highbarger's eyes burned with curiosity. "Well?" he asked, initiating our little game.

I hustled Maggie May out of the doorway and closed the door in the faces of the resident spectators. They had witnessed all I wanted them to see. The uniform escorted them to the lobby to wait for Crime Lab. Bullets Brown looked around. Highbarger waited.

Doc started the explanation of why we knew this was a homicide and not a suicide.

"The old man's been dead at least twelve hours," Doc began. "Probably more. That means he died late yesterday afternoon or early evening. Certainly he died before bedtime. A drunk might sleep in his clothing, but he'd probably remove his shoes."

I took over.

"Mr. Duke was right-handed. You can tell by the way he wears his belt, for instance, and the hip pocket he carried his wallet in. Now, look at the pillowcase. Duke being right-handed, the knot would likely have been on the *left* side of his neck if he strangled himself. It's on the *right* side. That probably means the man who strangled him was also right-handed."

"You never fail to amaze," Highbarger said.

"There's more."

I pointed to splatters of blood on the dirty sheet. A newspaper dated March 3, yesterday, lay on the bed. I lifted it to show how the droplets continued underneath the paper.

"The newspaper was dropped on the bed *after* Duke was murdered. Duke certainly didn't put it there himself. Also, that's not coughed-up blood from a ruptured trachea or something. Look. He was struck in the mouth and knocked back on the bed *before* he was strangled. Notice the angle of the blood spatter and its location."

It was Doc's turn again.

"A person committing suicide by strangulation," he said, "ordinarily uses a bath towel, a piece of bedsheet, a necktie—something long and slender that he can easily grasp. A pillowcase isn't long enough for a man to grasp and jerk tight enough to strangle himself. This old fart was killed by somebody in the heat of the moment who used the first weapon he could find."

"The motive?" I pointed at the dead man's gaping pocket.

Highbarger nodded. "Now, Columbo, can you tell me who did it?" he asked.

I smiled thinly. "In a short while," I promised.

Crime Lab technicians arrived with their cameras and powders and tapes. Doc and I examined the room with them inch by inch. Doc was the detail man, but I was the one who picked it up this time. There was a button and a cloth fiber on the floor. I squatted to look. Something else on the filthy carpet just below the corpse's dangling feet caught my eye. I carefully touched a shred of thin, partially-burned paper curled into a hollow tube less than a half-inch long. A few shreds of tobacco spilled onto the rug.

The dead man smoked Parliaments, not roll-yer-owns. Something clicked.

"Doc," I said, "do you remember the old whodunit movies where the bright young detective solves the case in a surprise ending in the vestibule?"

Highbarger looked bewildered, but Doc glanced at the home-rolled cigarette butt on the floor. A slow grin revealed the gaps in his teeth. I liked working with Doc as much as I did with McCracken.

Nobody said you had to play fair when it came to trapping felons. Over the years Doc and I together or singly had constructed some rather fantastic deceptions. The Grinning Hyena case with the "gay witnesses" was one of these. The other detectives were still chuckling over my most recent escapade with a gang of junkies who shot and wounded a druggist during an armed robbery.

After Detective Curt Hanks and I busted one member of the gang, the only clue we had to the remaining members was a scrap of paper in the captured one's wallet. On the paper was the name "Mark" and a telephone number.

I dialed the number while Hanks listened in on an extension. A man answered the call. I disguised my voice to sound like that of David, the bandit we had in jail. Never in a maggot's wildest nightmare does he expect a cop to call him like that. Besides, criminals aren't the smartest people in the world.

"Mark?" I asked.

"Yeah."

"This is David."

"It don't sound like David."

I jumped on him immediately. "What do you mean, it don't sound like David? What do you expect me to sound like when the pigs got me in jail?"

"What? Okay, David, take it easy."

"Mark, I can't talk long. But I got something you ought to know. The cops think you was with me on them robberies."

I could almost hear Mark's heart pounding.

"God, David!" he cried presently. "You didn't tell them anything about it, did you? You better not snitch, David. You keep your fucking mouth shut if you know what's good for you."

"Somebody's already snitching," I replied, putting a whine into my voice. "That's how they got me."

Mark cursed. *"Marty,"* he hissed.

I pretended to have a poor connection. "What?" I asked.

"Marty Johnson, that little prick. I knew that wimp couldn't keep his mouth shut. That chickenshit is as good as dead. If you say one word, David, the same thing'll happen to you."

"I ain't snitching, Mark. I ain't no Marty Johnson."

"Them dickheads questioning you about it?" he asked.

I glanced at Hanks on the other phone. He was

always so serious. He kept the bible in prominent display on his desk and wore a C.O.P. pin on his lapel—Christians On Patrol.

"There's two of them," I replied into the receiver. "One of them is tall and bald and ugly. Name's Hanks. Something like that."

Hanks slapped a hand over his receiver. I thought he was going to explode with laughter when I added, "The other one is young and good-looking with dark curly hair."

"What?" Mark said.

"You know, looks like one of them TV cops. His name's Sasser."

"Oh, yeah," said Mark.

Mark and Marty Johnson soon joined the real David in jail. By this time Mark knew it wasn't David who called him. I grinned when he sullenly refused to answer any questions.

"That's all right," I assured him. "You don't have to talk to me. If I need to know anything else, I'll call you on the phone."

It gave me satisfaction to outwit felons. There was one scene I had always wanted to play against a suspect in an investigation. The Cotton Hotel offered the only chance for it I'd probably ever get. Doc and I questioned the hotel residents for an hour, then I was ready.

"You know who the killer is, don't you?" Highbarger said.

I winked at him, then instructed Bill Houck the handyman to round up everyone in the hotel and have them meet me in the lobby.

"Yeah. Sure." He was off in a flash.

"He's the volunteeringest man," Doc commented.

Bullets Brown and Highbarger followed Doc and me to the lobby, where the Christmas tree had still not been taken down. It was brown and withered. The string of electric lights glowing in the wasteland only made it more pathetic. Needles falling on the spread-out newspapers below the tree made loud sounds as the hushed and wondering occupants assembled on that cold March morning.

It was an unusual gathering—the hotel manager with her crew cut, man's suit, and yellow tie; a horse-faced man; a paraplegic in a wheelchair; a fat woman twelve pounds heavier than a new Buick; drunks; pensioners; the handyman in his beige see-through nylon shirt; the other policemen looking more puzzled than ever. About twenty people altogether.

The dead man lay alone in his room with the door closed.

I looked around at the gathering and said, "I suppose you wonder why I've called you all here today?"

Doc turned away to hide his grin. I assumed a thoughtful pose with my hands clasped behind my back and slowly walked the length of the lobby that had now become my stage. Every eye followed. I slowly turned in front of the Christmas tree, stuffed my hands deep into my pockets, and surveyed the faces around me. Falling needles from the tree echoed in the silence. I played the moment for everything in it. All that was missing was a roll of thunder and a flash of lightning in the window.

"Someone in this room," I said, letting my voice rise dramatically, "killed Mr. Duke."

I had always wanted to say that.

No one moved. It was a frozen stage scene where the spotlight was on the main actor. David Highbarger was totally engrossed. We had played that little game of ours for years, but this was the first time he had participated in my investigation to this extent.

I started at one end of the ring of people, laying out a scenario as I worked my way to the other end.

"There are two entrances to the hotel," I began. "The back door is kept locked from the inside, so that you can go out but you cannot come in. Mrs. Maggie Catch was awake and in her office from the time Mr. Duke paid his rent yesterday afternoon until one-thirty this morning. Any visitors or strangers to the hotel had to come through the front door past her. There were none."

I moved slowly along the line, stopping here and there to continue my discourse.

"Our investigation tells us Mr. Duke died between four P.M. and six P.M. yesterday afternoon. The person who killed Mr. Duke was in the lobby when Mr. Duke paid his rent. The killer knew the old man was drunk and could probably not resist being robbed."

The suspense built. I moved on.

"Maggie May Catch and Gus Meadows were talking when Mr. Duke came in to pay his rent. Also present in the lobby were Delbert Jones, Claude Beasley watching TV, and Bill Houck."

I paused in front of Claude Beasley.

"Mr. Duke was drunk, so Maggie sent him to his room. But he came back to the lobby a few minutes later. Bill Houck told him he was nasty drunk and would have to leave. Claude Beasley practically had to carry the old man to his room. Claude left him sitting on the edge of his bed, where he was later found dead."

Every eye riveted on Claude Beasley, but I moved on.

"Some of you were in the lobby at all times until midnight, watching TV or talking. Like Maggie May, none of you saw any strangers or visitors. That means one of you in the hotel sneaked back to Mr. Duke's room and tried to get the old man's wallet. He wasn't so drunk, after all, that he couldn't resist. You hit him in the face. Then you panicked at the thought that Mr. Duke would report you. That was when you grabbed the pillowcase and strangled Mr. Duke to death."

I was enjoying the drama in a perverse way. I knew my suspect had to be sweating.

"This morning," I continued, "Bill Houck came running into the lobby and told Gus Meadows, 'Gus, Gus, come here. It's the old man. He's pretty bad sick.' Gus and Bill went back there and saw Mr. Duke lying across his bed. Bill felt the old fella's neck and said something like, 'His pulse is weak, but I think he's still alive.' He was already cold and stiff. Maggie May took one look and called the police."

Everyone was looking suspiciously at everyone else from the corner of his eye. The tension grew into something brittle. Doc edged around the outer part of the circle to block the door.

"The killer is standing among you in this lobby," I said. "Evidence tells us he is a short man with considerable strength. That means he is a relatively young man. He is right-handed."

I had almost reached the other end of the congregation. I let everyone listen to the Christmas tree needles falling for a moment. I was only two or three people away from my suspect. I saw him flinching at every sound.

I said, "The killer was in the lobby when Mr. Duke paid his rent. The killer is a resident of this hotel. He is someone you are so accustomed to seeing moving about the floors of the hotel that you don't pay any attention to him anymore."

It registered. Every eye immediately darted ahead of me and riveted on the man at the end of the line. I walked slowly to him and stopped. I thought Bill Houck would topple over from fright. He was short at five feet five, muscular, and at thirty-nine, the youngest resident of the hotel.

"Someone in this room killed Mr. Duke," I announced in a ringing voice. "That someone smokes roll-yer-own Prince Albert cigarettes."

Houck's hand flew to conceal the can of tobacco visible through his pocket. Color drained from his face. He became a mound of protoplasm. Highbarger shook his head in astonishment.

"You, William Houck, are the someone in this room who killed Mr. Duke!" I barked in my most dramatic tone.

Houck's body went into spasms. His hands, his legs, nothing seemed to work. His voice, when it returned, sputtered like a faulty engine: "But-But-But-But . . ."

He was still sputtering in his handcuffs when LZJ and Jack Powell entered the lobby.

"What's taking you two so long to work a suicide?" LZJ asked Doc.

"It's not a suicide," Doc said.

"It's a homicide," I added. "Here's your killer. Take him away. I think he wants to tell you about it."

William Houck confessed so readily to the murder of sixty-eight-year-old Theodore Duke that when Sergeant Johnson later cornered Doc and me, he asked, "What did you two do to that guy? He acted like he'd seen a ghost."

Doc chuckled. "What he should have seen," he said, "was some of the old late-night TV whodunits."

"Huh?" LZJ slicked down a loose hair.

"He didn't watch enough TV. He should have known the butler is always guilty."

Johnson shook his head and stalked away. "I'll never understand you two," he grumbled.

Only one question remained unanswered. I drove back to the Cotton Hotel. That Christmas tree had to be the most pathetic thing. It reminded me of a cur with terminal mange.

"It's March already," I reminded Maggie May Catch. "Why haven't you taken it down?"

Maggie May shrugged and adjusted her yellow tie.

"The tenants like it," she said. "It ain't much, but they say it makes the old place feel like home."

CHAPTER TWENTY-FOUR

Sometimes I awoke nights and sprang straight up in bed, sweating. I kept having the same nightmare. It started off with a perfectly normal human face. I didn't recognize the face at first. It was alive and laughing and talking. Then the face died. Lividity set in. It started to rot. The skin and flesh sloughed off. It wore this horrible grin.

Then I recognized the face. It was *my* face.

"Chuck, are you all right?" Dianne asked sleepily.

I was trembling. I wanted her to hold me real tight. "Di?"

"You're not getting enough sleep," she said.

I wanted her to hold me, but I couldn't ask. To admit to her or anyone else what went on beneath a cop's skin was a weakness. I was *The Man.* Twenty-four hours a day I was *The Man.* Even in bed with my wife I was *The Man.*

I told myself I was being foolish. I envied Doc Roberts sometimes. He was tough and his cop's second skin seemed to be thick and impervious to everything. He laughed in the face of it all. Death meant nothing.

Like the time he and I were attending an international homicide-investigation seminar at the University of Oklahoma. A pathologist conducted an in-class autopsy of some unidentified street person who died underneath a bridge or something and got his body donated to science. The pathologist opened the cadaver and sliced up parts of the body like cold cuts—the heart, the kidney, the liver—onto paper plates to pass around for examination. When the sliced liver came around, Doc held up a piece while everyone watched. He smacked his lips and popped the morsel into his mouth.

What no one knew was that the grizzled old cop with the missing front tooth had palmed a piece of *beef* liver before coming to class. It was the beef liver and not the cadaver's he slowly began to chew. That was the first time I saw *that* many tough homicide cops get sick all at once.

Doc was always coming up with something like that to demonstrate his contempt for death and his disregard for the sewer we walked through daily.

When a copy of a new Homicide Policy reached the chief's desk with a forged cover letter in Sergeant Johnson's name, everyone knew Doc's black wit had struck again. LZJ ran all over the station house ripping the missives from bulletin boards and office doors.

"What will the public think if they should get ahold of these idiot things?" he worried, red-faced.

Doc didn't even blink. "They'll think we have a splendid, caring leadership."

"I'll see if I can't increase your case loads if you comedians don't have enough to do."

Doc said that LZJ ought to have been a mortician. The sergeant was so hyper he had burned out every vestige of humor in his body. That made him Doc's ideal fall guy. He sputtered and almost went into apoplectic seizures after he stomped to his own desk and found there, taped to the wall behind his chair, yet another copy of the policy.

POLICY FOR HOMICIDE DETAIL

Homicide investigators should not:

A. Indulge in horseplay at death scenes by:
   1. Being a gooser or goosee.
   2. Telling ribald jokes in presence of decedent's family—especially jokes concerning the deceased.
   3. Draw mustaches, beards, and/or glasses on decedent's face.
   4. Let loud forensic windies.
   5. Lift decedent by hair or drag by one foot. (Dragging by both feet is permissible under certain conditions.)

B. Cause unfavorable publicity for Tulsa police department in presence of media by:
   1. Scratching and digging around certain parts of body when the TV cameras are on you.
   2. Picking your nose.
   3. Picking sergeant's nose.
   4. Leaving fly unzipped.
   5. Urinating or relieving oneself in presence of TV cameras. This is strictly forbidden.
   6. Tell newsmen and others you are the only one at scene who knows what he is doing.
   7. Tell newsmen and others you are the only one at scene who doesn't know what he is doing.

C. Cause embarrassment for Tulsa police department by:

1. Pronouncing live bodies dead and vice versa.
2. Drag racing with police vehicles.
3. Consorting with known criminals or shady ladies in police vehicles.
4. Taking naps at death scene, yawning, or otherwise seeming bored at death scene. Remember our motto: Every case is important to the victim.
5. Wiping blood from hands on suits or other articles of clothing belonging to Chief Medical Examiner or other detectives.
6. Informing any callers that one or all investigators are under their desks asleep.

D. Order autopsy on live person. A person may reasonably be assumed alive if he or she displays any of the following signs:
   1. Is still talking when placed on autopsy table.
   2. Heart beating.
   3. Breathing.
   4. Bleeding.
   5. Moving or thrashing about.
   6. Objects either verbally or in writing to autopsy. (Objections from decedent's family, whether verbal or otherwise, do not necessarily constitute reasonable grounds to believe decedent is not deceased.)

"How can you find that funny?" Dianne asked in disgust. "It's *sick.*"

Sometimes when the nightmare jolted me awake, I sat on the side of the bed and looked out the window onto the little meadow and thought I must be losing all capacity for human feeling and compassion. I kept remembering the homicide detective in Miami who arrived at the scene of where a girl had been raped and stabbed to death. Her nude body lay facedown on the sofa. Blood had soaked into the cushions and stiffened them. More of it, dark purple and lumpy from clotting, had pooled on the floor. The odor of blood in an enclosed space is cloying and sour-sweet. It made me feel a little nauseous.

The detective sauntered into the murder room with the manner of someone shopping for socks at a department store. He smiled and nodded at everyone, as though on a social outing. He bent over and peered indifferently into the corpse's face. It was like he didn't give a rat's ass.

"She must have been a pretty one," he declared. "What a waste."

He straightened up wearing a hard grin. He slapped the dead woman's bare ass with his open hand.

"Deader'n granma's clit, all right," he quipped, and laughed uproariously.

I thought him hard and mean and insensitive. Now, these years later, I was worse than that. If my cop's skin failed me and the shit did get through, it *still* wouldn't affect me. Maybe there was nothing left inside to be affected.

A thief got killed. His attorney was the mastermind behind a gang of thieves pulling high-dollar residential robberies on wealthy victims. An old man woke up to find a ski-masked bandit stalking toward his bed. The old man slept on a gun. He was a good shot. He drilled Roy Kennedy right through the ten ring. Don't tell me citizens shouldn't have guns.

"I applaud you for it," I said to the old man. "That was damned good shooting."

"I just pointed it," he said.

"You did good."

"But I killed someone. Lord knows I didn't want to have to do it."

"He was an ex-con who deserved it. Too bad you couldn't have drilled his attorney too."

One afternoon a man got shot in a downtown shootin' gallery. The call came out as a suicide. Patrolmen were holding two women and a man at the scene. One of the women was going ape. All she wore was her panties. She kept screaming and rolling her eyes back toward the dead man on the bed while the uniforms tried to calm her by making her look out the window onto an alley.

The other young woman had sunk into a doper's haze. She sat cross-legged and naked on the floor smiling at motes as she picked them out of the air. Her arms, the backs of her hands, and the big veins in her neck were scabbed with needle tracks.

Her boyfriend smoked a cigarette and watched her. He wore a pair of ragged jeans. His hand shook so hard that his cigarette smoke described erratic little etchings in the fetid air.

In the midst of smoking grass and glassine bags of brownish-white powder, burned spoons, matchsticks, and needles that littered the room lay the dead man on the bed next to the door. He lay on his back, naked, with his legs spread. The body was still draining. The head was on the edge of the bed and the blood ran out of the hole on the lower side in a thinning stream and splashed on the floor. It sounded like a leaky water faucet.

A .44 magnum makes a big hole going in and coming out. Some of the guy's brains were on the ceiling.

The two couples had been smoking weed, mainlining smack, and playing switchies or something. Our hero, now dead, produced the .44 magnum revolver just like the one Clint Eastwood as Dirty Harry in the movies used when he said, "Make my day." The .44 had been stolen in a house burglary the week before. He took all the bullets out of the gun except one and boldly announced that *he* had the balls to play Russian roulette.

You could have stuck a flashlight through the hole in his head.

"I was wrong," Doc said. "Justice doesn't necessarily have to come from the barrel of a *cop's* gun."

The patrolmen were laughing. The bumper sticker stuck on the wall above the dead man's head said: I'LL GIVE UP MY GUN WHEN THEY PRY MY COLD DEAD FINGER OFF THE TRIGGER.

I grinned. "Pry that cocksucker's cold dead finger off the trigger."

Doc Roberts started a tally of all the corpses in the city. He called it his death inventory. He said someone died in Tulsa every hour. Died, got killed, or killed himself. That meant 24 stiffs a day, 168 a week, 672 a month, 8064 a year.

"I knew a corpse cop who once kept a list of all the names of the DOA's he worked," Doc said.

"What on earth for?"

"To remind him," Doc said.

"Remind him of what?" I asked.

"Our ultimate destination—just another piece of meat that somebody has to clean up off the streets."

You could often find a human heart, or an eye, or a liver on Dr. Leo Lowbeer's desk in the pathology lab at Hillcrest Hospital. A woman, accidentally killed by her husband practicing his fast draw with a loaded

Colt single-action revolver, turned out to be pregnant. Doc Roberts was always helping Lowbeer dig around in bodies. The two of them brought something out to me and dropped it in my hands. It resembled a little crystal ball. Inside it was a fetus about two or three inches long. It had a head and rudimentary arms and legs and was all curled up inside the clear ball.

"The stupid sonofabitch killed two with one bullet," Doc said.

He had had his wife stand in front of him with her palms apart. He slapped leather and tried to thrust the gun barrel between his wife's hands before she could clap.

He drilled her through the heart.

I studied the fetus for a long time. This would have been a *real* human being in another few months. Perhaps, I thought, it was better that it died. It might have grown up to be a thief or a murderer. There were already enough of those living.

I gave the little clear ball back to the gnomelike pathologist. He placed it on top of his desk among a clutter of blood-smeared papers. It remained there for the next two or three days, until it dried up and began to smell.

Doc Roberts never missed an opportunity to help Lowbeer with an autopsy. The two baggy men bent over the long stainless-steel tray, cutting open the corpse, while the doctor went on and on in his heavy German accent, lecturing. Doc worked and listened. Doc knew more about anatomy than many real doctors.

They performed the autopsy on a white WWII combat veteran shot and killed by a black street gang on the northside. An autopsy was required on the body of any victim of violent death; it had to be proved in court that the victim died of gunshot or stabbing or whatever and not of some sudden natural causes.

The five black teenagers involved in the murder were tough and all doped-up and swaggering shoulder to shoulder down the middle of the street, blocking traffic. The veteran yelled at them to let him pass. The teenagers yelled back and started throwing rocks. The veteran jumped out of his car. One of the kids shot him a couple of times with a .22 Saturday Night Special.

The triggerman was seventeen. I found him and eventually sent him to the joint to join his father, who was serving time for having previously shot and killed the boy's mother.

Dr. Lowbeer used a tiny electric saw to make a cut completely around the dead veteran's skull just above the eyebrows. He removed the skull top like you might take off a yarmulke. The brain was pinkish-gray and resembled the two halves of a huge English walnut. The pathologist scooped it out and handed it to me to examine. It was heavy.

A human looks strange with the top of his head and his brain missing. He looks like a house without a roof. Doc and the pathologist bent over and peered into the empty cranium. Lowbeer pointed out nerves and sinus passages and the backs of eyes.

Two hours ago this man had been alive in North Tulsa. He had dreams and thoughts and loves and hates and got hungry and felt the sun and the rain and had been loved and went through a war and paid his bills and taxes and . . .

I held his brain in my hands.

How quickly it all ended.

Death didn't mean anything. Not really.

I placed the heavy organ on a stainless-steel table and walked out. Doc and Dr. Lowbeer were still busy. I washed my hands and went outside into the sunlight and across the street to a little park. I swung in a children's swing and looked up past the green trees to the sky and the clouds. I watched people walking by. Children were playing in the park.

Death didn't mean anything. You could hold a person's brain in your hands. It wasn't anything at all.

CHAPTER TWENTY-FIVE

Whenever I felt my cop's skin growing thin and the case load heavy, I tried to escape by driving to a place I knew on remote Haskell Lake several miles south of Tulsa. It was a small lake, maybe twenty acres, girded by low banks of rock and jumbled boulders with a flat at one end filled with sawgrass, cattails, and lily pads. David was reaching an age where he liked to fish, as I always had as a hill kid growing up in the Ozarks.

Almost no one followed the potholed dirt road to Haskell Lake. I didn't want to see anyone when I was there.

Winter was going to come early. Cool September nights persuaded the cottonwoods and blackjacks rimming the lake to avoid the last-minute rush in donning autumn colors. The cottonwoods turned a rich gold. Scarlet leaves burned fiercely here and there among the green of the blackjack oaks. Armadillos and skunks rustled last fall's soft carpet of dead leaves. It would soon be replaced by a new, noisier carpet. A pair of southbound mallards caught the fading sun, with the drake's green head and the hen's pattern of black zigzag on brown.

David and I fished the lily pads for largemouth and bluegills. After nightfall we fried fish over an open fire. We had fried potatoes, too, and a can of pork 'n' beans washed down by Pepsi kept cool in the lake.

Later, in our sleeping bags, David felt talkative. At eight years old he wasn't always the chatterbox his little brother Michael was.

"Daddy? What's *that,* Daddy?"

"An owl, Big Dave."

"Daddy, it's *dark.*"

"It's always this dark at night, Dave. Look up through the trees at the stars."

"Daddy, do other people live on the stars?"

"I wouldn't be surprised if they did. What do you think?"

"Are they . . . Do you think they're *monsters,* Daddy?"

"Monsters live only in people's minds, son."

"If people live on the stars, what do they look like, then?"

"Maybe they have one leg or four legs or a dozen eyes or something."

"Daddy, can we get up real early in the morning and fish before we go home?"

"That's why we come to the lake."

"Daddy, 'member that big bass I caught up here last time? I caught him all by myself, didn't I?"

"You sure did. He was bigger than mine."

"Daddy, how come nobody but us comes here to fish?"

"Maybe not many people know about it."

"Maybe they're scared of *ghosts.*"

"I think mostly they're scared of being alone."

"Were you ever lonesome, Daddy?"

"Sometimes."

"Was that before you met Mommy?"

"Mostly."

"Does Mommy like you, Daddy?"

"I hope so."

"Do you like her?"

"She's your mother, son. I married her."

"Does that mean you like her?"

"Yes."

"I heard you and Mommy talking. She said you wasn't happy 'cause you can't be married to the police and her too. Daddy, I don't ever want to be married. If I become a policeman too, can policemen live with their mommies and daddies?"

"You can live with us as long as you want."

"Daddy, did you ever shoot anybody?"

"Yes."

"Did he shoot you too?"

"Are you warm enough, David?"

"Can we come and sleep on the ground again?"

"I promise. We'll camp out lots of times."

"Daddy, do you know something? Good things happen, don't they?"

I watched his sleeping face in the moonlight. Then I got up and made my way down to the low bluff by the lake and sat there watching the water gentle in the night. I didn't want to, I fought it, but I still got to thinking. It was warm out, but I shivered anyhow when I saw in my mind's eye the little rice-wad of maggots in Suzanne Oakley's ear that morning at the morgue. That led to other somber thoughts of death and violence. I tried to fight them off, but it was like being mugged.

I saw the mouse darting out of the bloated corpse's mouth. I saw maggots glued like softballs to the heads of people who had blown out their brains. I smelled the death rot from the morgue . . .

I shook my head hard to clear it, but the home

horror movie of grisly mutilated faces and bodies kept running. I sometimes joked about death being contagious. Maybe it was, in a way. Sooner or later death caught up with us all.

I tried to explain to Dianne once how I was feeling. "All I see is the dying and the violence," I said. "It makes me think every day that I'm dying too."

I might have gone on to tell her about the nightmares, except I recognized the horror in her eyes.

"You don't have to stop," she cried. "You can talk to me."

It was too late. "I did talk to you," I said lamely.

"That's not talking. I want you to share things with me."

I looked at her. "You don't want to share *these* things with me," I said.

Sitting in the moonlight by the lake, I felt the presence of a kind of terror growing inside me. It was like the nightmares I had. I had those nightmares when I was asleep, but now I was awake and having them. It felt like my skin was rotting off the bones. I had to look to make sure it wasn't. I felt alone and small and mostly alone because a cop was always alone and could not touch and be touched and still be a cop.

I grasped my legs and pulled my knees up to my chin and dropped my head onto my arms. And then, alone, I cried for a very long time and never ever told anyone about it.

CHAPTER TWENTY-SIX

Gail Farrell was a young farm girl who grew up poor and went barefooted and hiked up her dress to wade streams. When she was eighteen, she married an older man, a farmer, and lived with him in semi-isolation on his dairy near Lake Keystone west of Tulsa. One Wednesday near midnight she had a quarrel with her husband. Fuming, and naive like many farm girls, she took off on foot to walk and hitchhike the twenty miles to her sister's house in Tulsa.

Her first ride, a man and his family, let her off at the Keystone Expressway that curved in a wide loop along the Arkansas River and through Sand Springs before it entered Tulsa. She started walking between the distant night lights that marked the expressway. It was midweek and late and the traffic was light. The highway cut through sparsely settled countryside. It was a dark, desolate stretch of road.

Gail almost turned back and went home, but she was angry and had committed herself. She gamely trudged alongside the road. Several headlights swept over her and on past before a light blue vinyl over dark blue Chevrolet Malibu pulled off the road ahead and waited for her to come running up. It was occupied by one man. He swung the passenger's door open for her. Before she climbed in, Gail looked at the driver. He was dark-haired, in his thirties, with the makings of a pot gut like that of someone who drank too much beer.

He smiled at her.

"You're lucky," he said. "I come along this road every night on my way to work."

He introduced himself as Tom. Gail clambered into the car with him, and the conversation remained light and friendly for the first few miles. Then, suddenly, as they approached the outskirt lights of Sand Springs, Tom appeared to undergo a strange metamorphosis. The smile vanished. He glared at Gail with such open hatred that it was almost as though he'd slapped her.

Frightened, Gail spotted a freeway exit.

"This is where I get off," she said. It wasn't, but now she wanted any excuse to get out of Tom's car.

Tom pierced her with his smoldering eyes. "Girls shouldn't walk," he said. Even his voice had changed. "They should stay home where they belong."

"No, Tom. Really—"

His hand snapped out like a striking snake and caught her arm as he swerved off at the exit. She tried to break free, but he almost yanked her arm out of its socket.

"I did you a favor," he snarled. "Now you're going to do me one. I don't mean to hurt anybody, but don't get me angry."

Trembling with terror, Gail sat trapped in the car as Tom selected an isolated street and drove toward the Arkansas River. Gail took a deep breath and tried to regain her calm in order to reason with the stranger. The vise on her arm increased its pressure. Her arm went numb. The Malibu entered a tiny isolated park that overlooked the river. There were a couple of picnic tables, a children's swing set. Almost no illumination from the city entered the park. Everything plunged into darkness when Tom parked underneath the trees and doused his headlights.

Gail heard the flow of the river. Moonlight gleamed off its surface. There was a beadlike string of house lights glittering on the opposite bank almost a quarter mile away across the water. Gail's heart thumped in her chest. She thought she would faint when Tom turned his eyes on her. They glinted like marbles.

It took all the effort she could muster to keep from panicking. Thinking he would kill her if she struggled, she sat in the car in the darkness while her body slowly turned into a block of ice. Instead of assuaging her fears, the calm voice that began to rumble out of the man only increased them. He talked for an hour on a series of disjointed unrelated topics. Although he remained calm, his madness cut into his captive like the thin blade of a sharp knife. Gail concentrated to keep from doing something foolish to set him off.

"Do you believe in God?" he asked. "All my wife does is go to church. She doesn't have time for me. She is either in church, watching television, or doing television exercises."

Tom's grip on Gail's arm seemed to relax as time passed and she did not struggle to escape. Gail let him talk on while she carefully looked around to select an escape route if the opportunity presented itself. She realized with a cold sinking feeling that no one was likely to come to her rescue at this time of the night.

Tom said, "I want to take you home. My wife will understand. We'll lock you in the bedroom and keep you there."

His grip relaxed more. Realizing that she might not get another chance, Gail took a deep breath and in the same movement lunged for the door handle and attempted to jerk free of Tom's grasp. A scream tore from her throat.

Too late she realized she had underestimated the man. His fingers closed in a steely grip on her arm. He yanked her against the car seat and methodically pummeled her with his fists until she gave up and lay quietly. In a few minutes he let her sit up, but he continued to hold her arm. Gail tasted blood from where he split her lip.

"You're not really hurt," he crooned. "You're okay. I didn't hurt you."

Then he looked away. He looked sad.

"She hit me and she shouldn't have done that," he said. "She should never have done that."

Gail didn't know who he was talking to; she didn't know what he was talking about. They sat in silence a moment. Gail cowered as near the door as his grasp on her arm permitted.

"You know," Tom mused presently, "I had a dog a long time ago. It bit me. It shouldn't have bit me. I took my knife and stabbed it."

Gail was desperate with fear. "Please, Tom, I—"

He backhanded her hard across the face.

"Don't call me Tom," he admonished. "Call me Tommy like my mother used to."

"I'm going to start screaming if you don't let me go."

He looked at her with his eyes like marbles.

"You wouldn't want to do that," he warned. "Have you ever took a pig and hung it up by its heels and cut it from its throat all the way down to its heels? They bleed a whole lot of blood. But God understands. He knows when I do that. He understands and He loves me."

The laughing cackle he emitted might have been the most terrifying thing yet. He continued his high-pitched cackling sniggering while he forced Gail onto the seat and brutally stripped her jeans to her knees. She tried to resist, but he was too strong for her. He struck her in the face repeatedly with his fists. He cackled and raved and chattered like someone insane as he mounted and raped her.

"They knew they should have stayed home," he chortled. "If they had, they wouldn't have got hurt. Oh, well. God forgives everybody. God knows what I'm doing, but I'm not doing anything."

His teeth sank into her cheek, bringing blood.

"I want to be a cobra and bite through to the blood."

He slugged her in the face with his fist.

"There! There!" he exclaimed. "That feels good."

Afterward he permitted Gail to sit up while he buttoned his trousers. Battered and bleeding, the young woman huddled sobbing on her side of the car with her jeans around her ankles. Tom stared at the river in the wan moonlight. Gail's hand crept toward the door handle. He no longer held her arm.

"The river," he said. The way he said it made Gail tremble. "I know. You should be in there."

He reached underneath the seat.

That gave Gail the courage and desperation to try again. She grabbed the door handle. The door flew open. Her jeans were around her ankles, but she managed to dive free. She rolled on the ground, jumped up and ran, yanking at her jeans. She heard Tom's car door open, running footsteps. She tumbled behind a downed tree near the river and attempted to make herself a part of its shadow.

For Gail the next half hour was the longest of her life. She heard Tom scurrying around in the park furiously kicking at bushes and screaming threats. She feared he would hear her heart thumping against the ground. She dared not show herself to try to outrun him.

"I'll find you if it takes all night. I'll find you, and when I do you're going to bleed."

He swept within a few feet of where she huddled like a terrorized rabbit in the tangled branches of the felled tree. Not daring to even breathe, she buried her face in her hands and felt the wetness of silent tears. She expected brutal hands to reach into the tanglefall and grab her.

She expected never to see another day.

Tom charged a noise in the opposite direction.

"I heard you! You're going to bleed! You're going to bleed!"

Teenagers entering the park to watch the river in the moonlight and neck likely saved the woman's life. Alarmed by the approaching headlights, Tom jumped into his car and squealed out of the park. Gail collapsed in great racking sobs of relief.

I listened so intently to Gail Farrell's story, although she fumbled through it looking embarrassed and humiliated, that by the time she finished I was leaning across my desk toward her. I sank back and caught my breath. I looked away while Gail fidgeted and waited. I suspected that if she had not retained her wits and managed to escape, we would have found *her* body in a park on the Arkansas River with her throat slit and maybe her nipples cut off and jammed up her.

The first thought that entered my mind was: *I got the sonofabitch.*

It *had* to be him. Statements Gail Farrell attributed to her attacker flashed repeatedly through my thoughts, like beacons guiding me into a harbor after a long and trying voyage.

They knew they should have stayed home. If they had, they wouldn't have got hurt.

They? Geraldine, Marie, and Suzanne? Who else.

You're going to bleed! You're going to bleed!

Had he also muttered those words to Martin, Rosenbaum, and Oakley—just before he killed them?

From what Gail described of her attacker, he even fit the profile Dr. Kinsey had drawn up so long ago. From Kinsey came: *The man . . . has a long list of hang-ups which he has never been allowed to vent.*

I discerned in Gail's description a man full of hang-ups about his mother, his relationship with his wife and women in general, and about God.

He hates women, Kinsey said. *He probably has been rejected by women in a dating or marriage situation.*

If he is married, he may well have a very stormy relationship with his wife.

The rejection by his wife, the stormy relationship—it was all apparent in Gail's narrative about the man who picked her up on the expressway.

At last, I was so near Jekyll and Hyde that I could almost smell him.

McCracken was ready to jump on it. "This time, Columbo, you've got him."

"I don't know."

I still didn't dare hope, not after all the others.

"I think Dianne will be glad to see this over with," McCracken said.

"Yes," I said. "Yes. *If* it's him."

"It's *him,*" McCracken almost shouted. He drew vigorously, enthusiastically, on his cigarette, making the tip glow fiercely. "Goddamn, Sasser! You always said you'd do it."

I was almost believing it myself. I chanced a grin. Weights seemed to be disappearing from my shoulders.

"Then let's go get the shitbag," I said.

CHAPTER TWENTY-SEVEN

Before you catch a criminal, you build up in your mind a caricature of a subhuman type who is somehow *different* from ordinary mortals. You think that for him to commit such a horrid crime he has to be bigger and meaner than your next door neighbor. Evil incarnate does not come in size medium or Sunday Sears. My Mr. Hyde *had* to look like something out of the early horror films of Hollywood in order to justify my long preoccupation with him.

But then after you catch him, you're always disappointed. He turns out to be a miserable, scruffy little bastard who whines a lot and makes excuses. It's like you're always fishing for trout and catching tadpoles.

For a week McCracken and I scouted the sprinkling of tiny towns and communities that bordered Lake Keystone—Mannford, Pawnee, Kellyville, Jennings, Lotsee, New Prue—searching for "Tom" and his blue over blue Malibu. For a couple of hours each night we staked ourselves on the Keystone Expressway near where Gail Farrell had been picked up, attempting to catch Tom on his way to work. I was so wired by growing expectations that my long pursuit of Dr. Jekyll and Mr. Hyde was about to end that I could not sleep even when I went home. I dragged out all the old reports and started rifling through them. I wanted to be prepared when I had Tom in front of me in the interrogation cubicle.

I kept thinking of previous killers I had arrested, like Mike Brown, Richard Harris, and Jim "Grinning Hyena" Walsh, who had murdered, been released from prison or escaped, only to murder again. I secretly entertained the hope that Tom as Mr. Hyde would resist arrest and I could end once and for all any legal technicalities of his being released back into society to renew his reign of terror. Like cops always said—the only justice there is comes from the barrel of a cop's gun.

"I feel it," I explained to Dianne. "I'm closer to catching him now than ever before."

"There'll just be another case to take its place," she said.

"No."

I looked at her a long minute.

"I'm thinking about quitting the police," I said. "It's destroying me."

That was the first time I had openly admitted that the shit was seeping through my cop's skin. I expected Dianne to be ecstatic. Instead, she showed no emotion whatsoever. It was like she didn't care anymore. Maybe it was too late for her to care.

"What will you do so you can make as much money as you do now?" she asked uninterestedly.

I didn't bother to reply. I walked away.

Police Chief Ted Blackburn of tiny Cleveland, Oklahoma, provided the key to solving the mystery. He said a man named Tom Gifford drove a two-toned blue Malibu and worked the graveyard shift at a Sand Springs machine shop.

"I've noticed he's been driving his wife's car to work, though, for the past week or so."

That was why we hadn't spotted his Malibu on the expressway.

Rather than waiting for Tom to feel safe enough to start driving his own car again, I sneaked up to his house in the darkness an hour before he normally left for work and sabotaged his wife's car so it wouldn't start. I wanted to arrest the suspect out of his own car to make sure we had no legal difficulties impounding it to search for pubic hair, blood, and other evidence of the crime.

Then McCracken and I waited on the Keystone Expressway for him to drive by on his way to work. I whipped my unmarked in behind the Malibu and radio-directed a nearby uniform car to redlight him. I made it a flying stop. Like I said, you're always disappointed after you catch your suspect. The man I jerked from behind the wheel was a pudgy, relatively short man of thirty-five with dark, frightened eyes and a cowlick. He reminded me of Richard Harris, the Mohawk Park killer. He had the same black hair, pale skin, and little paunch.

"You're under arrest for first-degree rape!" I barked as I spread-eagled the man against his car and applied handcuffs.

His response came spontaneously: "Which one?"

McCracken grinned and nodded. He mouthed the words: *We got him.*

Hours later, weary in the time just before dawn, McCracken slouched at his desk with a cigarette and a cup of black coffee. I lifted chin from chest and peered at him across the quiet space that separated our desks. McCracken slowly turned in his chair and gazed out the long narrow window onto Fifth Street. He drew deeply from his cigarette and didn't say anything. I dropped my head onto my arms and immediately fell into a troubled sleep.

When LZJ arrived and heard the news, he nervously slicked down his hair.

"He's got to be the one," the sergeant declared.

I hitched up my trousers, tried to brush some of the long-night wrinkles out of my jacket, and started to walk off.

"Columbo!"

I wheeled, flaring, "Goddamnit, Johnson. It's not him either, okay? We've been locked in that fucking room with him since midnight. He's even passed a polygraph. He's a rapist and we *could* have had another dead girl in the park—but he's *not* my Jekyll and Hyde."

"Sasser?" Sergeant Johnson ventured in a different tone of voice.

"Larry, I don't want to talk about it. We're going home to get some sleep."

"Are you all right, Sasser?" LZJ asked.

I had never seen him concerned about any of his men before.

"I'm fine, Larry. Why the hell shouldn't I be?"

Immediately, he was the old LZJ again. "Columbo, where's your reports?" he asked.

I dumped a pocketful of matchbox covers, old envelopes, and other pieces of paper on my desk. All had been scribbled on. LZJ shook his head as I walked out of the detective bullpen and took the elevator down to the parking lot. Dark thoughts of a Jekyll and Hyde who couldn't be caught intruded into my mind. No matter what I had told Dianne, I knew I couldn't quit the police until after I caught the man who brutally raped and murdered my three girls.

"You got him?" Dianne asked when I walked into our living room and slung my jacket and shoulder holster over the back of the sofa. The boys had just caught the bus to go to school. Neither of them had even *started* school when I began the Jekyll-and-Hyde investigation. As far as they could remember, I had always been working it.

Dianne saw the answer in my face. She turned and went into the kitchen to get breakfast started. I dropped my head on my chest and leaned against the wall. I felt the terrible chill of silence.

CHAPTER TWENTY-EIGHT

Being a cop was hard on marriage. Almost every cop I knew had been divorced at least once. It came with the badge. Married over twenty years, Doc Roberts had a girlfriend on the side; the end of the year would find him divorced. Bill and Pam McCracken's marriage was bouncing off the rocks. McCracken a time or two had casually mentioned that he was thinking about resigning from the P.D.

When I came home from the streets or from working my extra job teaching Criminal Justice at the college, I came home to a silent house. My sons were generally in bed asleep, and Dianne was sleeping on the sofa with the TV going or in the bedroom underneath the covers with her back turned to my side of the bed.

Sometimes she just pretended to be asleep. She didn't want to make love to me. She didn't want to hold me.

"You're not romantic. This is the way you touch me."

She pawed her body in a coarse imitation of foreplay. I blushed from pain and embarrassment, turned my back and sat on the edge of the bed and glared out the window at the moonlight.

"It's like I'm living with someone who has no emotions," she said. "I think you've forgotten how to feel. You're just a shell. You're empty."

I wanted to do things that would make her want to hold me. I tried to show her I wasn't empty.

"Words mean nothing," I explained. "Actions count more than words. Didn't I build you a new house? Don't I work two or three jobs so my family can have things? I'm not out hanging around bars and running around on you. Doesn't all that count for something?"

It was quiet on the ranch with just the horses around and no sounds of traffic and no near neighbors. The moon shined through the bedroom window, beyond which I could see the spindly arms of the pole corral and the forest on the hill where I used to like to watch the sunsets and the rainbows after a shower. I hadn't stopped to watch a sunset or a rainbow in a long time.

I slumped on the edge of the bed in the moonlight, gazing out the window while Dianne either slept or pretended to sleep. I wanted desperately to be held. I wanted Dianne to turn over and hold me very close and make the streets go away. But there was no reaching. Months passed, and there was no reaching. There was just the cold moonlight on the bed with Dianne's back turned to me. The streets and that other world separate from her and our sons were a reality from which there was no escape.

I knew my friends were experiencing the same kinds of things. Half of them drank too much. They were cops, and they went to off-duty watering holes to forget they were cops. It wasn't to be long before Officer Bob Fagen parked his patrol car at the station on a night shift and smoked his service revolver. "I just couldn't live with it any longer," he wrote in his suicide note. Monte Peterson still called me sometimes to be her rainbow.

I ached from loneliness. The nightmares were so real that I could smell death, even with my eyes open. I thought if I closed my eyes I might not open them again. I didn't want someone like Bill McCracken or Doc Roberts or Bunny Brown coming out and throwing the sheet off my stiff corpse and tossing me around to see if I had a .22 bullet hole in the hairline at the base of the skull or a needle mark in my jugular. I didn't want a homicide cop handling me like I handled so many others, and then going and washing his hands because he'd handled me.

I thought about my dead cop friends—Ron McLeod, who took a robber's bullet in the brain; Vic Butler, ambushed and riddled with slugs in the Miami ghetto we called The Zoo; Thurman Spybuck, the narc who got his during a gunfight at a westside doper pad; all the others killed in car chases or accidents or fights. One of my rookies I trained to the streets when I was in uniform got shot through the gut. He stood in front of a screen door on a routine disturbance call, and a dirtbag came to the door and shot him through the screen door. When I reached Intensive Care at Hillcrest, Freiberger had hoses and tubes running out of every orifice. The bullet entered near his navel and exited a quarter inch from his spine. He could have been a vegetable for the rest of his life. He grinned feebly when he opened his eyes. He tried to reach for my hand. I grasped his hand and held it hard. No words are needed between cops.

Later, he said, "You're right. A man can get killed in this business. Is it all worth it? Does anybody give a damn?"

Soon afterward he answered his own questions by resigning from the P.D. and going to work for the telephone company.

Whenever I thought of the job and death, my thoughts invariably turned to Jekyll and Hyde, as though drawn there by a powerful magnet. His presence accompanied me wherever I went, it came to me in my sleep, it taunted me.

"*Nobody* should be able to commit crimes as horrible as this and get away with it," I said. "He's still out there somewhere. He can't escape forever."

"Bingo!" McCracken said.

"I just can't let go," I confessed. "Somebody has to care."

"Maybe he's left Tulsa," McCracken reasoned. "Maybe he had a conscience after all and committed suicide and now no one will ever know the truth. Maybe he got killed in a car wreck. Maybe he's in the joint serving time for other crimes."

"Maybe I'll catch him tomorrow," I shot back stubbornly.

Dianne was always watching me. "It's become an obsession with you," she accused. "Why is it so important for you to catch this one killer? You've caught so many others."

It *was* important, that's all. I continued my desperate search, running down violent sex criminals, scanning reports and newspapers for a connection between my three girls and the nation's burgeoning number of serial killers. In Texas a farm worker confessed to having slain twenty-seven young boys whom he enticed into homosexual acts. A New York postal worker who called himself the Son of Sam stole out into the streets at night to murder because his dog told him to do it. A mortician kidnapped women and left their dismembered bodies strewn about—a head at the front door of a police precinct, a hand in a worker's lunch box, a trunk on an elderly couple's front yard. In California maggots calling themselves Satanists were sacrificing babies and virgins.

"It must be getting hard to find a virgin anymore," Doc Roberts said.

McCracken broke his wrist in three places when he went in with me after a suspect who locked himself in a bathroom. I was kicking the door to break it down and my partner got his arm caught between the door facing and the door. I heard the bone cracking. I kicked in the door and made a swipe at the scroungy little pervert. The scuffle ended with me knee deep in a filled bathtub holding the suspect under and near drowning him while I snapped on handcuffs.

I bristled whenever I got near the maggot low-lives who victimized people. I felt the hate inside me growing day by day, like a fast-moving disease that rots as it spreads. I *hated* criminals. We caught them, and the courts and corrections let them out, we caught them again, and *again* the system let them out to continue their victimization.

When I found myself surrounded in a house full of thieves and dopers, among them the murderer of an elderly woman tortured and electrocuted, I managed to get the word to McCracken. Like the ex-Marine he was, he kicked the front door off its hinges and burst in alone with a shotgun at port arms. I was sitting in the living room playing it cool with my feet propped up, keeping the punks at bay with a barrage of words. I grinned around at the assemblage of maggots, who still hadn't tried anything because they weren't sure why I was there questioning them. Then I grinned at McCracken.

"It's about time, William," I said. "All these cocksuckers are under arrest. Shoot the first scumbag who runs for it—and I hope somebody tries."

A one-armed would-be rapist who assaulted women

in Laundromats attacked me with a knife when I went out to bring him in. A Peeping Tom threatened to get out of jail and kill me. I outran on downtown city streets a freak who was breaking into houses, stealing women's lingerie, and defecating in the middle of his victims' beds.

LZJ looked worried. "Columbo, take McCracken or Roberts with you from now on."

"I'll let you know when I need somebody, Johnson."

The other homicide cops waited and watched.

"Columbo, you have no evidence," they said. "How are you going to prove it's him even if you do find him?"

"I'll know it's him," I said. "I'll prove it. There are ways to get justice."

There were two separate worlds for me, and they seemed to be merging. There were the streets with their murderers and thieves and dopers and freaks, and then at home there was the cold moonlight on the bed and Dianne's back turned to me.

Snow lay piled on the sidewalk on Christmas Eve, and it was starting to snow again. It was almost dark when I left the police station. Downtown was decorated with Christmas lights, and people were bustling about, getting in their last-minute shopping. I stood outside on Fifth Street in the snow and pulled my tattered black trench coat close around the sweater and sport coat I wore underneath.

The cold seeped all the way to my core. I shuddered and started to turn to go to my VW, parked in the lot. I paused and looked around. I didn't want to go home. I couldn't go home to that bed with the cold moonlight on it.

I ached for someone to hold me against the cold.

I had never done anything like this before in my marriage, but now I did. I telephoned Wanda, one of the secretaries at the D.A.'s office. She was cute and tiny, with bobbed dark hair and a miniskirt.

"Chuck?" Surprised. Then her voice lowered on the other end. "What is it?"

Before I could reply, I heard her off the phone explaining the call to her husband.

"It's one of the detectives asking about a charge," she said, her voice muffled. "No, hon. Crime doesn't stop just because it's Christmas."

She came back on the phone.

"I don't know anything at all about the Smith case, Chuck," she said, for her husband's benefit. "Did you talk to Yolanda? The last I heard the charges were being typed and . . . Okay, he left the room. You devil! You'll be working a homicide at my house."

I took a deep breath and blurted it out: "I called to ask you out for a Christmas drink."

She hesitated. Then she said, "I've thrown myself at you like a streetwalker for months. All I got was teasing. Are you teasing me now?"

"I'm as serious as a heart attack."

"But it's Christmas Eve."

"I know it's Christmas Eve."

"How am I going to get out of the house?"

"You can handle it."

"What if Wally gets suspicious?"

"It has to be tonight," I said.

She paused on the other end of the line. Then she asked, "Where?"

We met in the parking lot of the shopping center at Thirty-first and South Sheridan. She drove up in her Thunderbird, slipping and sliding on the fresh snow. Sand trucks were clearing the lot and streets for late shoppers. I had stopped at a liquor store for a pint of gin. I had never cheated on Dianne before, not in twelve years of marriage, and I needed the liquor. I took what was left of it with me when I jumped out of my VW and Wanda moved over to let me behind the wheel of her T-Bird.

She laughed and pulled open her coat to reveal a tight, shiny black jumpsuit set off by high heels, and a Madonna on a wide black ribbon around her neck.

"I'm a flirt, and everybody thinks I'm going to bed with all the assistant D.A.'s," she confessed, "but this is the first time I've gone out with anyone except my husband."

"Why me?" I asked.

She sobered. "There's something very different about you," she said slowly. "You seem to be so tough, but you're as vulnerable as a little boy beneath it all. If anyone can ever get through to you. Anyhow, I just wanted so badly to go with you that I couldn't say no. I never thought you would call me. I could have fallen over when I heard your voice, except Wally would have wondered about it."

I drove the T-Bird across the Arkansas River to a secluded bar and club in West Tulsa called Li'l Abner's.

"Can you park in back?" Wanda asked. "Somebody I know might drive by and recognize my car."

I kissed her before we got out of the car. I kissed her deeply, but I felt nothing. She clung to me. I pushed her away.

"It's Christmas!" I whooped. "I want to dance in a corner and rub your splendid butt and get gloriously drunk and make love to you. I don't want to be cold ever again."

Afterward we drove to Lake Keystone and parked and I took her in the backseat of the Thunderbird with the windows fogged from the heater and her legs spread so that one was thrust up the back of the seat and the other stretched out on the floorboard. Our movements kept rapping her head hard against the side.

I drove in silence on the way back to Tulsa. Wanda perched on the space between the bucket seats and traced circles on my cheek and played with my hair.

"Columbo," she said when we drove back into the shopping center parking lot. It was very late. The stores were closed. My VW was the only car in the lot.

"Don't call me that," I protested.

"Everybody calls you Columbo."

"I have a name of my own," I said. "I'm not just a cop. I'm a *real* person too."

"Why are you suddenly so touchy?"

"I'm not touchy." I cut the engine next to my VW and closed my eyes. I was still cold.

"Chuck, I think I could love you."

My eyes popped open. "Don't ever say that. There is no such thing as love."

That struck her like a blow to the face. She collapsed into the bucket on her side of the car. Tears glistened in her eyes. "You mean this was just a one-night stand? That's all you wanted?"

I looked away. "I guess that's true," I admitted.

"You were just using me."

"People are always using each other."

"You get a piece of ass and that's all you wanted." She sounded bitter from more than just tonight.

I started to tell her I wanted something else, but I didn't know what it was and I hadn't gotten it anyhow.

"Chuck, you're a bastard. You're like every other cop. I was wrong about you. You don't even have a heart."

I sat there a minute gripping the steering wheel.

Then I said, "Yeah," and jumped out of Wanda's T-Bird and got into my own car. Wanda was still sitting there crying when I left in the snow. I flipped on the radio. Elvis Presley was singing, "It's a little more like Christmas . . ."

I kept shivering all the way home.

CHAPTER TWENTY-NINE

They were a pair of lards. Their thighs rolled together when they walked. Shirley Cook resembled a fat penguin in her one-piece black-and-white swimsuit when I tracked her down to the YMCA pool. She wasn't going to talk to me about Harold Doak. "He'll kill me sure if he finds out I'm snitching." She started to waddle away.

I knew how to get a reluctant witness's attention.

"You either talk to me," I called in a level voice, "or I toss your fat ass behind bars as a material witness to homicide."

You couldn't have mouth-plugged Shirley Cook and her girlfriend Sammie Lintonberg and shut them up after that.

"Harold's really weird," Shirley Cook said. "He burns candles, sits in trees, puts spells on people in the moonlight. He goes to Satan conventions and tells everybody he's a warlock."

I looked at her.

"Well, he *does!*" she cried.

Sammie Lintonberg's statement was even more

bizarre. Her eyes rolled when she talked, and little self-indulgent smiles creased the fat on her face. She was so grossly fat she hardly had facial features. "Little asshole eyes," Doc Roberts said when he saw her.

"Harold is morbid, intelligent, and evil," Sammie Lintonberg monologued. "He's fascinated with dead people. Like, he lives across from a graveyard. He always said how appropriate he lives there because he always wanted to dig somebody up. He asked me if I would dig up somebody with him, and I said no! He talked about sacrifices, but he never really told me about one.

"He tried to strangle me once, though. We was, like, drinking and smoking pot, and went to bed. We had sex and Harold wanted a blowjob, but I wouldn't do it. He said he could tell what I was thinking. Like, we was laying there and he got on top of me and started strangling me. He said I was thinking he was the one who killed them girls. I almost passed out, but I broke his stranglehold. Then he started hitting me. He said he was sorry after he got done."

"Just because he choked you doesn't mean he killed the three girls," I pointed out.

"He *told* me he killed them," Sammie Lintonberg said, wide-eyed. "Do you remember when that jogger was killed in the park? I seen Harold after that, and he had scratches all over both arms. I asked him about them, and he said, like, he'd better watch out or the police would think he was the one going around murdering girls. Then he laughed about it.

"Later on, like, we drove off the road in Sandy Park by the river and got stuck. We was sitting there listening to music and a weird song came on. Harold said, 'I have something I want to confess to you.' Then he said, 'I murdered those girls. Don't you never tell nobody or I'll murder you too.' He said it and he meant it."

McCracken was ready to go to the D.A. right away with the information. Doc Roberts noticed my troubled expression. "The Fat Girl Syndrome?" he asked, rubbing his chin and looking wise.

Several years before, Doc and I were investigating the death of ten-year-old James Riley Woollum, who had been strangled and left naked in a patch of woods in southwest Tulsa. We had an apparent witness, a fat girl who reminded me so much of Sammie Lintonberg they could have been twins. This girl laid out in careful detail how her boyfriend tied her up and made her watch him murder the child. The entire thing turned out to be the product of her imagination. Since then, Doc and I had called the phenomenon the Fat Girl Syndrome—fat girls of low esteem who discovered they could get all kinds of attention by coming forward with outlandish tales of murder and mayhem. That was what bothered me about Sammie Lintonberg.

"She *could* be telling the truth," I decided. "The world's weird enough for *anything.*"

At thirty-five years old and barely five feet tall, Harold Doak was an evil dwarf of a man with a disgusting alive mouth that drooled and crawled and sagged all over his face, and out of which escaped a kind of slithering, sniggering sound. His police rap sheet included at least thirty sex-crime arrests —indecent exposure, sodomy, child molestation, window peeping—and first-degree burglary. Jess McCullough had dragnetted him in for questioning when Geraldine Martin first disappeared. He sniggered and slobbered when McCracken and I found him denned up in a dilapidated rooming house on

North Peoria Avenue. He lived off welfare checks and food stamps. The government took care of its "victims of society."

"The police know my record," he said. "The police know I get caught on indecent exposure or for letting some dude go down on me in the park, but I ain't no killer. Look at me. Do I look like I'm big enough or strong enough to kill anybody? I'm just a sex freak. The only thing I want to do is stick a hard dick in something."

His room was littered with porn—paperbacks, magazines, tapes. His closet was stashed waist high with materials Doak created himself—elaborate sexual cartoons drawn in colored pencil, cut-out nudes from magazines arranged and pasted in new and imaginative positions, fantasies laboriously hand-printed to look like printed booklets. His main theme dealt with a skinny, humiliated-looking man exposing an enormous penis to an array of buxom Amazons, who pointed at him and laughed.

"My psychiatrist says it's good therapy to sketch out my fantasies," Doak explained. "He says that way I won't be tempted to go out and act them out."

I could imagine the dwarf locked inside his dingy room hour after hour toiling over his craft, sniggering and drooling like some demented miniature Frankenstein.

"Does it work?" I asked him.

"Fuck! What do you think? It makes me want to go out and do it more."

I dragged Doak in, and for the next two days went at him in one of the little interrogation cubicles where so many killers before him bared their souls. When Jack Wimer picked up the news, the *Tribune* blared the headlines: TULSAN JAILED IN DEATH OF WOMEN. Citizens telephoned to say how relieved they were that the Jekyll-and-Hyde killer had been captured. The Gray

Ghost awaited word that I was ready to go to the D.A. with the case. LZJ said the mayor and the governor called.

"They're on my ass," he said.

By the second morning I despised Doak's snigger. I despised the perverted dwarf who made that disgusting sound and who seemed willing to talk on and on. I soon knew more about him than his state-paid psychiatrist knew. For twenty years the state had been sentencing him to probation for his crimes in order that he could be "treated" and "rehabilitated."

"Sandra," he said of one woman with whom he had lived after moving out of the house where he'd lived with two fags named Stan and Montie, "is a short, dumpy little broad with a face like a ugly baby. She introduced me to sadomasochism. She liked to get beat. She didn't get much charge out of just my hand, so I kept her all bruised from the belt. I started trying to get rid of her. Who wants to make love to a chick that's all battered up? I don't mean I was going to kill her. One day I came home and she'd left a note saying she was going to Houston with a big dude with a big belt. I was glad she left.

"Sammie Lintonberg, the cunt. She and that friend of hers named Shirley. Them two are really weird. They like to hang around cops. One night they drove me out to Kip's Big Burger on Harvard. They were smoking pot and drinking and hollering at policemen. After I ate, I made an excuse to go to the bathroom. I climbed out the bathroom window and left them there. They're gross as puke, with personalities to match.

"I tried to show Sammie how to be more seductive. We were talking about how unresponsive she was. I wanted her to whip me and give me a head job. She wouldn't do it. She just wanted to fuck straight. I didn't strangle her. She's lying if she said that. I grabbed her and told her to get that shit out of her head about fucking straight. I told her if she was the only chick in the world, ugly as she is, I'd turn queer."

I sighed wearily. "Aren't you?"

"I'm bisexual. I'll fuck almost anyone or anything, but not *her.*"

Dianne stared at me when I got home. I collapsed in bed from the mental and physical strain. The chase for Jekyll and Hyde would soon enter its fifth year.

"Chuck . . . ?"

"I'm so damned tired of it all."

Back at Harold Doak again the next morning.

"I never told Sammie Lintonberg I killed anybody. I wouldn't tell her *anything.* She's a cop groupie. She can't keep her mouth shut. *She's* the one that talked about murder all the time. She kept saying to me, 'Harold, you might be the Jekyll-and-Hyde killer.' I told her, 'Yeah, if I was, you'd be in trouble.' I put her and Shirley on about the witchcraft shit because they like to hear about it. I think Sammie's trying to get me in trouble because I won't have anything to do with her. She's a liar. She couldn't tell the truth if her fat hog's ass depended on it. The cunt."

Sammie Lintonberg refused to take a polygraph test to prove she was telling the truth. So did Shirley Cook.

Harold Doak was guilty of all kinds of misdemeanors and felonies. He kidnapped and molested an eight-year-old boy. He broke into houses and masturbated on women while they slept. He sneaked around in the dark and peeped through windows. He prowled parks and waved his wand at little girls. But he took a polygraph test about the Jekyll-and-Hyde murders—and passed it.

"I ain't never killed nobody!" he shouted in exasperation and fatigue. "But you ain't gonna believe me, are you? I'm tired of this shit. I didn't do it, but you got your mind made up. You might as well file on me and get it over with."

He collapsed with his chin on his chest, his disgusting lip drooling. I climbed slowly to my feet. I studied him for a long minute. Everything about him revolted me. If perversion could be personified, it would look just like him.

I sighed deeply. The man wasn't a killer; he was a worm who would rather be beaten than beat someone else.

"You're the asshole of the world," I told him. "You dirty up the streets like dog shit, but I want you out of my sight when I open that door."

Snigger snigger. And he was gone. Back into the sewers.

The scar on McCracken's lip turned as white as wax against his flushed face.

"You let the fucking killer go, Sasser!" he accused angrily.

I turned and walked off.

"He did it, Sasser. Goddamnit! How could you let that maggot go? Sammie Lintonberg has no reason to lie on him."

LZJ looked worried. "I'm catching heat from the brass, Columbo. They're on my ass. *Could* he have killed them?"

"*You* could have killed them."

"How can you be so sure Doak didn't do it? The D.A. would file. Let a jury make the decision."

"Doak didn't do it," I said flatly. "I want the *right* Mr. Hyde when I catch him."

"You're never going to catch him," LZJ said.

Dianne didn't have to ask. I sank onto the sofa and stared at my feet. Michael came and sat close to me and put his head on my shoulder and patted my arm. He was seven years old. It was hard to believe I had pursued Mr. Hyde for most of the boy's life.

I thought I saw tears in Dianne's eyes.

"How much longer can this go on?" she said in a very sad and tiny voice.

CHAPTER THIRTY

Bill McCracken wouldn't let Sammie Lintonberg and Harold Doak go. He said he was going to resign from the police department, but he didn't want to leave when he *knew* Harold Doak was my Jekyll and Hyde. As for Sammie Lintonberg, she kept feeding McCracken's convictions. She seemed as determined as McCracken to make the police believe Doak killed Martin, Rosenbaum, and Oakley. Every week or so LZJ tossed another police report at me describing Lintonberg's crusade.

> Reporting officer was radio assigned in reference to a disturbance. Arrested at the scene was Sammie Lintonberg for assault and battery. While en route to jail, Ms. Lintonberg stated she could produce the weapon in the Marie Rosenbaum murder case if she didn't have to go to jail. She stated she had been told by Harold Doak of the murder and had even helped him get Rosenbaum's body over a fence, because he couldn't do it himself, due to his small size. She also stated that prior to getting the body over the

fence, she had seen Doak slice the body completely down the back with a knife.

"Sammie knows the details on the murders," McCracken insisted hotly. "I think she was with Doak when he committed all three."

"She's a liar," I said.

"How do you *know* that?"

"Her lips move."

Reporting officer was approached at the YMCA by Sammie Lintonberg, who stated that the reason Miss Oakley was killed was that she was a sacrifice and that Harold Doak had been the actual perpetrator of the crime.

McCracken's face flamed. "Just because we call you Columbo doesn't mean you're always right," he snapped. "You're overlooking the killer. It might be your case, but I'll go over your head to get something done if I have to."

LZJ was getting nervous. "Are you sure Doak had nothing to do with the murders?"

Even Investigator David Highbarger of the Medical Examiner's office, who had never questioned my judgment before, lifted a quizzical eyebrow. "Are you sure? Are you *really* sure?"

McCracken was closer to me than a brother, but I knew I couldn't back off the stand I had taken. A jury, if it believed Sammie Lintonberg, might actually convict Doak. While Doak was a scumbag who deserved to go to the joint, he didn't deserve to go for a crime he hadn't committed. The affair was placing a severe strain on a friendship I valued.

I proceeded to the address of Sammie Lintonberg, who stated she could take reporting officer to a location where a knife had been stashed by Harold Doak which had been used to inflict mortal wounds on a sixteen-year-old runaway by the name of Marie. Miss Lintonberg stated that Doak had committed this homicide sometime during August, in basically the same area where Suzanne Oakley was killed.

I proceeded with Miss Lintonberg to a location where she pointed out a spot where the knife was buried. There was nothing found at this time.

"Doak moved it," McCracken raged. "Sasser, you're so fucking stubborn, you wouldn't change your mind even if you knew you were wrong."

One morning LZJ handed me a letter scrawled on brown business paper. Sammie Lintonberg's name appeared on the return address. The envelope had been opened in the chief's office.

"The chief thinks McCracken might be right," LZJ said. "He wants it checked out further. Sammie Lintonberg *could* have been there when Suzanne Oakley was murdered."

I am going to write it just as it happened. Met Harold at Keith's about 8:00 P.M. We took five hits of speed. We were at the bar till about 11:00 P.M. Went back to hang around the Y. Walk over to Civic Center and talk about stuff till nearly 3:00 A.M. Walk and bought some beer and started to walk to the railroad bridge. Finished the beer. Got in a fight. He slap me and I got mad. He hit the beer bottle against the bridge. Broke it. Slashed my wrist. He got sort of crazy after that. It was bleeding really bad. He wiped the blood on his shirt and said, "You'll see blood if you stick with me." We walk further down the path in

River Park and sat down by those trees. He started talking off the walls. I guess I was too. We saw her coming. He jump and said, "Here is your chance to see all the blood you want."

There was another person with us that we met on the bridge. I think his name was Wes. He was Indian. Harold went up to her and ask her for a match. She said she didn't have one. He ask her if she would like to smoke a joint. She said, "No." He hit her in the mouth and threw her on the ground and drag her by her hair down to where me and Wes were. She was screaming and crying. I got scared and tried to run up the hill. Wes grab hold of me and held me on the ground. Harold held her down while Wes held me down. They took off their belts and tied me to a tree and told me that I better keep my mouth shut and my eyes open. I didn't try to get away. Harold started to beat her with his cane and Wes was laughin'. It all happened so fast. I thought that's what they were going to do to me. But I got those belts loose and ran. They didn't try to stop me. I had blood on me from her and my own blood from my wrist.

"She's all fucked up," I said.

"Sasser, you're the best homicide detective I've ever seen. But you could be wrong."

"I'm not wrong."

I took my weekend off and returned to work. When I walked into the bullpen, McCracken glanced away, then got up to walk out.

"William . . . ?"

The tall man paused at the door with his back to me. "Partner," he said, "I'm doing what I think is right."

He left the bullpen. I was still bewildered by

McCracken's odd behavior when LZJ came to my desk and sorted through the clutter. He pointed to a file folder.

"If you'd clean up your desk, you'd have found it," he said. "Read it. McCracken and Roy Hunt took another statement from Lintonberg. When Sergeant Hunt comes in for his afternoon shift, he and Bill are going to the D.A.'s to file murder charges against Doak."

I looked at LZJ.

"It seems like a good case," he said.

I was too outraged to speak. I read the statement quickly. I exploded. "This is no interrogation. They lead the bitch through it like a dog on a string."

Doc Roberts lit a cigarette. His movements were measured; he had that mischievous look in his eyes. "This statement is like the murder lineup Craig County held for us last week," he said.

LZJ jerked a hair out of place and had to slick it down quickly. "I don't want to hear any more of your barnyard philosophy, Roberts," he growled.

"It's germane," Doc replied, and went on. "Before they started the lineup, the deputies brought all the witnesses in and introduced them to the stand-ins that were going to be in the lineup. Damned if one of the witnesses *still* didn't pick the wrong man. The deputies almost shit. 'Oh, no, ma'am. That ain't the killer at all. Don't you remember? He works upstairs in the clerk's office. We introduced him to you. Now look at that other man over there. See him? That one. Now ain't he the one you seen running away?'

"This statement is just like that lineup. You make sure it turns out the way you want it to before you ever start it."

LZJ rubbed his face hard. He hated to get thrust in the middle of something. "What do you want me to do about it?" he asked.

"I want you to go to D.A. Buddy Fallis and tell him."

Johnson blanched. "I can't do that."

I hiked up my .357 and started out of the bullpen.

"What are you going to do, Sasser?" LZJ called after me. "Don't get your ass in a crack. Or mine either."

It didn't take me long to run down fat Sammie Lintonberg.

"Man, like, I ain't going with you. You let Harold go."

"Get your fat ass in that goddamn car."

Then I radioed McCracken to meet me. I had to do what I had to do, but I was deriving no satisfaction from it.

"Sammie and I have a little demonstration for you before you go to the D.A.," I told McCracken.

He looked puzzled but no less stubborn as I drove the three of us to the little clump of undisturbed bushes and trees in the park. When we got out of the car, Sammie looked around, blinking. I glanced at McCracken. He was watching me with a kind of reluctant curiosity. I turned to Sammie.

"Where were you sitting with Doak and Wes before this all started?" I asked her.

"You don't believe me," she whined, turning to McCracken for rescue. "You think I'm a liar."

"Show me!" I barked.

She flinched and jumped back. After a moment of blank staring, she led the way down a little knoll to a spot near the trees.

"Now, point to where it was on the bicycle path that Doak attacked the girl."

She pointed. The bicycle path was eighty feet away.

"Doak went up to the girl when he talked to her, right?"

"Y-Yes."

"What was it again that he said to her?"

"He asked her for a light, and then he asked her if she wanted to smoke some pot."

"You were right here and heard him?"

"Yes."

"Stay here," I ordered. "William, come with me." As we walked to the bicycle path, I added, "William, think carefully about what you're going to see before you go to the D.A."

We stood in Sammie's plain view on the path, looking back at her.

"Would you actually screw that filthy pig?" I asked McCracken.

"What are you doing, Sasser?"

"She is a fat, sloppy, dirty, smelly, *lying* pig."

I smiled and waved at Sammie. She waved back. I saw McCracken understood. I shouted down at Sammie, "You heard me, right? What did I say?"

"You asked if he had a light," she shouted back. "Then you said, like, 'Do you want to smoke some pot?' "

I looked at McCracken. "That's just the beginning," I promised, and for the next half hour I led Sammie Lintonberg through her paces.

"Did you *see* Harold stab Suzanne Oakley?" I demanded.

"No, man, no."

"Sammie, you don't have to be embarrassed. You can tell the truth. You saw him stab her *there,* didn't you?"

"I was scared, man. Like, I tried not to look. But I seen anyhow. I seen him stab that girl. He stabbed her in the pussy."

Suzanne Oakley's wounds were all in the throat and left breast.

"Get it all out, Sammie," I encouraged. "How many times did he stab her?"

"I only saw once. Then I wouldn't look anymore."

"Sammie! Tell the truth."

"Man, okay. Like, I was looking. I saw him stab her three times in the pussy."

"Was that when you ran away?"

"Man, I was scared."

"But then you came back to see, right?"

"He had a spell on me."

"Sammie, tell the truth. You never even left, did you?"

She hung her head.

"Why did you lie about Wes being there with you?"

"I thought you'd see I was telling the truth about Harold if somebody else was there too."

I kept at her, giving her no relief, leading her wherever I wanted.

"Harold never carries a knife in his pocket," I said. "Where did he get the knife? Did you give it to him?"

"The knife was in Harold's cane. It was one of them canes with a knife in it. There was lots of blood."

"Did he stab her before or after he butt-fucked her?"

"That was before. He had a gun, man, and, like, he held it on me while he fucked her."

Something perverse in me wouldn't let McCracken off until I was sure I had demolished any lingering expectations he might retain about his case against Harold Doak. He had become tight-lipped. Red crept up his neck.

"Sammie, Harold made love to you first. Didn't he, Sammie?"

She batted her eyelashes. "I wasn't going to tell you about that."

"Isn't it also correct that you had sex with him *after* he killed Suzanne?"

"He wanted a blowjob, but I wouldn't do it."

I smiled grimly at McCracken. He averted his eyes and silently gazed off toward the river. I made Sammie change her story several more times. At one point she was saying Harold made her clasp her arms around a tree where he could watch her while he had sex with Suzanne's corpse. McCracken finally stopped me.

"You've made your point," he conceded. "It still doesn't mean she was lying about everything."

I wasn't feeling good about what I had done to him, but I said, "There won't be any charges filed, William. You either go to Buddy Fallis and tell him what happened here today—or I'll tell him. And from now on, stay out of this case. I'll handle it."

McCracken turned and walked to the car. I felt that emptiness inside me start to expand.

"William . . . ?"

He kept walking.

William McCracken didn't tell me he had submitted his letter of resignation. He came into the bullpen one morning and turned in his badge and gun and emptied all his personal papers out of his desk. I watched him. I always felt uncomfortable when such a large man looked beaten. He made his way slowly toward my desk.

He smiled with that old laconic twist of his scarred lip. "You'll never clean up your desk, will you, partner?"

"William, I'm sorry about Doak and . . ."

The thought of the incident, I saw, still pained him.

"You were right about me, Columbo," he said. "I jump to conclusions like a duck on a june bug. I was never the detective you are. I never could be. But I made a good sidekick, didn't I?"

"The best there is, partner. Wasn't it you who solved the Richard Harris case?"

He smiled thinly. "If you jump often enough, you're bound to get the right june bug occasionally."

We were both uncomfortable with our emotions.

"Partner," he said, "I guess I just wanted to end the Jekyll-and-Hyde case for your sake, before the god-damned thing kills you. Fuck Harold Doak. He's a maggot. I'd send the cocksucker to the electric chair and strap him into Ol' Sparky myself if I knew it'd free you."

Then, alone, his suitcoat trailing from his hand, his holster empty, William McCracken walked out of the police station. From a window, I watched him pause in the sunlight that lay across the parking lot. He looked around for a minute, expressionless, before he climbed wearily into his private car and drove away.

CHAPTER THIRTY-ONE

I was *The Man* now for nearly fourteen years, seven of those as a homicide detective. I had seen kids boiled in water. I could eat a hamburger in the same room where a softball of maggots worked over a bullet wound. I had killed and it didn't bother me, and I could do it again if necessary and then go out and laugh about it over a drink with another cop. I had my second skin to keep the shit off, but I also had that recurring nightmare about dying.

"You're not the same man I married," Dianne kept saying. "You're hard. You won't let anyone near you, not even your own sons. You have your second skin—and it's made a prisoner of you. God, how sad."

One afternoon I came home from a shift and walked into the house. Dianne came quietly down the hallway. She was freshly showered and pretty. I watched her, wanting to say something light and clever to make her laugh, trying to clear my thoughts of a case in which an eleven-year-old northside kid beat his three-year-old cousin to death with a belt and then tried to cover up the crime.

Eleven years old.

Dianne came up to me.

"I want a divorce," she said.

That was all she said. I looked at her, trying to protest it, wanting to beg, but unable to form any response. Speechless, I simply turned away and walked out of the house and found my way to the corral. I had to have something alive to touch. There was always the stallion Storm that I had raised from a yearling and trained. I pressed my face against his neck underneath the long mane, and that was the way I stood for a long time while I tried to slow down the world and put it right side up again. I stood there desperately holding onto the horse, still with the big .357 tugging down on my entire body. I couldn't cry. *The Man* never cried. There was just a dryness, an emptiness.

David was eleven years old. Michael was eight. I had always tried to protect their mother and them.

After the divorce they went away with Dianne, back to Florida. Before they left, David clung to his mother, and Michael—chubby, dear little Michael—hugged me and ran behind the house to keep me from seeing him cry. He thought that was the way it was supposed to be, that a man never cried.

The bitterness erupted from inside me like rot from an apple's core. I had never drunk much before, but now I did. I looked around me and all I saw was death and evil and filth and scumbags. That was my world, a black and seamy place in the gutters and sewers of society. My family had been my island, albeit a precarious one, and now I had lost even that. I found myself immersed in a world I despised completely because it seemed completely corrupt.

"I'm going to kill a maggot today," I said when I

awoke in the morning, often with a hangover, and strapped on my big .357 to go to work.

Maggots were corrupting the world.

"Justice is a cruel joke," Doc Roberts said. "Criminals victimize people because they know society will not retaliate."

I drank and then I said, "I'm going to kill a maggot. Justice comes from the barrel of a cop's gun."

Mr. Hyde was a dead man if I found him.

McCracken located me at a Brookside bar on the Restless Ribbon. I had rarely carried an off-duty gun, not since Miami, when it was required, but now I did. It went with me wherever I went. McCracken came in and sat down with me in a dark corner where I was drinking beer and staring into the glass.

"Have a beer with you, partner?" McCracken asked.

I looked up. I hadn't noticed him come in.

"It's a free fucking world, William. How did you know I was here?"

"I used to be a detective."

He sat down. A beer came. I said to him, "I suppose I'm a *real* cop now."

Cops always said you weren't a *real* cop until after you killed a maggot, got divorced, and became an alcoholic.

McCracken drained his beer in one gulp, ordered another. We sat there across the table from each other and looked at each other. It was hard for me to see his pain because of my own pain. Finally, he looked away and his scar got white the way it did whenever he was suppressing emotion.

"Pam and I are getting divorced too," he said.

I didn't know what to say, so I said, "William, it is one fucked-up world."

"Tell me about it."

"Do you want to talk about it?" I asked him.

"Do you?"

I drank. "I guess we don't," I said.

"Partner," McCracken said. "I'm your friend."

"I'm your friend back, William."

You don't have to say much when you're talking to another cop.

What I had contracted was a dreadful weakness, and any display of weakness was something other cops avoided like it was the bubonic plague. I could have told them it was something that happened to all of us sooner or later, that we were all vulnerable to it in our own time, but those who hadn't experienced it didn't want to believe it, and those who had, didn't want to see it again. Doc Roberts, anticipating his own divorce, passed by my desk in the bullpen, grasped my shoulder, and kept on walking.

I made LZJ so nervous he kept watching me and slicking down his hair.

"Put somebody in jail, Columbo," he said, trying to break through.

"Don't call me Columbo."

"Come with me, Chuck. I'll buy you a cup of coffee."

"You still don't know I don't drink coffee."

"Just come with me."

He drove, following the city's network of expressways.

"Sasser, everybody's talking," he said when he could finally think of an opening. "The brass is down on my ass. They're afraid you're going to do something stupid, like when Van Winkle was off-duty and killed the maggot in the bar."

Van Winkle would have gone to the joint if it hadn't

been for my intercession. It was stupid on his part, but it had still been self-defense.

LZJ took a deep breath. "The chief wants me to put you behind a desk for a while."

I shot him a quick, sharp look.

"Just until everything settles down," the sergeant interjected. "Then you'll be right back."

"Johnson, I've worked major crimes for fourteen years. You're not putting me on the rubber-gun squad."

"You got it wrong, Chuck. It's only temporary."

"I'm not riding a fucking desk, Johnson."

"Listen to me. You're not doing your job."

I shook my head. "How long have I worked for you, Johnson—six, seven years?"

"I've always said you were the best homicide detective I ever knew."

I made LZJ uncomfortable. It was like he was afraid he might catch whatever it was I had.

"Know what I like about you, Johnson?" I asked sarcastically. "It's your loyalty. The only fucking thing you care about is what the brass says. You got your nose so far up the chief's ass, I'm surprised you don't suffocate. I work my butt off all these years, and then one little thing comes up and you want to shitcan me."

LZJ looked hurt. "You might not believe it," he said, "but I'm thinking about you."

I jabbed my finger in his face. He swerved the car.

"Get this straight, Johnson. I'm not burnt out. I'm not getting off the streets, and I'm not leaving Homicide until I catch that cocksucker."

"What difference does it make?" he shot back, then looked quickly away before I saw the chink in his own armor. He pulled to the roadside and parked. "Sasser, when you come right down to it, what's so important about catching Jekyll and Hyde? There are so many others that'll take his place. You'll get headlines in the papers for a day or two and then everybody'll forget all about it. That's just the way we are. Nobody really cares. I'm willing to bet you can't go out right now in Tulsa and find one person out of ten thousand who remembers the names of all three girls—Martin, Rosenbaum, and Oakley. I'll go further than that. I'll bet you can't find ten people in the whole city who remember.

"Chuck, don't you get it? Nobody gives a damn. Nobody really cares for justice or right and wrong, and it simply keeps getting worse. Nothing you or anyone else can do will ever make a difference. Don't try to be Sir Galahad, Sasser. There aren't any noble knights anymore. You just end up being Don Quixote jousting at windmills while everybody laughs at you."

I stared at him. This was a side of LZJ I had never seen before. Was it because he had also been hiding behind his own thick cop's skin?

"One man," he said, "can never make a difference."

McCracken had always said that, and then he proved it by resigning.

"Johnson, don't you dare jerk me off the streets. I can make a difference if I catch him. It makes a difference if I keep the scumbag from killing somebody else."

"Did it really make a difference when you caught all those other killers over the years? Did it really? Could you tell any difference in the world? It just doesn't mean anything."

Everyone in the system was saying the same thing, maybe just in different ways. A friend of mine, Rick Peters, was an assistant warden.

"Offenders don't mind coming to prison," he said.

"It's like a short vacation from the rigors of committing crimes. In prison, they don't have to work. They don't have to worry about bills and insurance. They get free medical and dental care, three hot meals a day, clothing, a place to sleep. They don't even have to do their own laundry. And even the worst among them sooner or later gets to go home on weekends and holidays.

"It's a system created by lawyers for the benefit of lawyers. They're involved in every step of the process. They judge, defend, appeal, appeal again, and file against the system to make it ever more lenient. The more lenient the system, the better job security it is for lawyers. Nobody else really cares. You can't change it. Nobody can."

Like Doc Roberts said—*we put 'em in, they let 'em out.*

No one can make a difference. *No one.* And no one cares. None of it means anything. For fourteen years I had fought it out in the streets, trying to make a difference. The crime rate was almost double what it was when I wore that zoot suit to the Miami police oral board. I *was* Don Quixote.

"I have got to make a difference," I told LZJ.

A few nights later I chased a fleeing fugitive on foot across the parking lot of the Safeway store at Third Street and Utica Avenue. Marie Rosenbaum had been abducted from this lot. It was after midnight and the streets were virtually abandoned. I had my .357 in my fist. I felt the rage inside me boiling as we pounded down an alley and I cornered the scumbag against a building. We faced off at each other, both of us panting from the fast, hard chase. The guy was a tall black man in his mid-twenties with bulging muscles and a broad sloping forehead. Defiance was written all over his face. We were one on one in a dark alley. The guy obviously meant trouble.

"You puke-white honky cocksuckin' muthafucka," he snarled, and spat a gob of shit at me that splattered on my shirt front.

I felt a coolness, like a sudden temperature lowering, in the pit of my stomach. All the rage was gone. I even smiled as I took a step forward, lifted my revolver slowly, and pointed it at the bridge of the man's nose. The revolver remained steady. I was still smiling.

"I be walkin' out over the top'a your white ass," the dude said, but his voice didn't sound quite as cocksure as before. "You won't be shootin' none'a me, muthafucka."

I had no feelings at all. It was like I was empty, like I was mechanical.

I said, "You won't be walking out of here at all."

There was no one else around, just him and me. I slowly pressured the trigger. The hammer started back.

"What you think you doin', muthafucka?"

All I had to do was testify that he, a wanted felon, resisted arrest.

I kept smiling.

The dude's eyes popped wide. They cast back the distant yellow glow from a streetlight. I picked out exactly where I wanted my bullet to go. I *could* make a difference. At least *this* scumbag would victimize no further innocents.

"Good night, cocksucker," I said, ". . . and goodbye."

The hammer was about to fall. It was my own voice, clear and loud suddenly in the night, that stopped it, and it was the unexpected memory of another time when I was going to kill the man who raped his six-year-old daughter. I had promised myself then that it would never happen again, that I would never let the shit penetrate my cop's skin to touch me personally. Now, here I was—a homicide detective about to commit homicide. I caught people for this and put them in prison.

My cop's second skin was gone, worn away by years in the streets.

My gun hand started trembling. Seeing that, the maggot's scorn returned to ride his face like a triumphant jockey. Maggots in the streets were as contemptuous of weakness as cops were.

"Honky muthafucka . . . I be goin' right over your stinkin' ass like a dose of salts."

The man would never know how close he'd come to being dead. I eased the hammer down on the revolver. It was still an effort to keep from going through with it. I was trembling all over. As the dude came toward me, I reached as far back as I could with the heavy weapon. It split the air in a shrill whistle as I brought it around with all the strength I could put into it. I felt the barrel bury itself into skin and flesh and bone. The man dropped to the ground like an empty sack.

The next day I went to LZJ. I was still shaken by the events in the alley. I had made a decision.

"Larry, take me off the streets. I'm turning in my letter of resignation. I don't want to be Columbo anymore. I don't want to be The Man."

Geraldine Martin, Marie Rosenbaum, Suzanne Oakley. I couldn't bring them back. They were dead. There was nothing I could do for them. Besides, maybe LZJ and the other cops were right. Maybe it didn't mean anything, maybe no one cared. Maybe one man could not make a difference—*except within himself.*

There, within myself, I could make a difference.

There, I *had* to make a difference before I became a kind of Jekyll and Hyde too, as bad in some ways as the man I had been chasing for the past five years. I knew I had to let him go in order to save myself.

I just wouldn't think about it anymore.

The killer, if not stopped, will kill again.

AFTERWORD

Monte Peterson always called me her rainbow.

"People need a rainbow sometimes. You are my rainbow."

One evening after I had been away, I came back and someone gave me a clipping from the second page of the newspaper. Cops who shoot themselves seldom make front-page headlines.

POLICEWOMAN FOUND DEAD OF GUNSHOT WOUND

> Tulsa Police Lt. Monte Kay Peterson was found dead of a gunshot wound to the head in her house at 4:45 P.M. Friday, police said . . .

That was another thing *real* cops did—smoked their service revolvers. Monte was getting divorced. We had had pizza together the night before and I brought her a rose.

"Chuck, I need a rainbow."

Few of the rookies came to Monte's funeral. There were just the seamed and hardened faces of the cops from our generation—the police lieutenants, sergeants, and detectives. They sat silently in the pews and no one showed emotion. You didn't show emotion if you were a cop. You were *The Man.*

I was no longer a cop.

I walked down the aisle of the chapel to Monte's casket. I placed a single red rose next to it. Monte always liked me to give her a rose. I didn't care who saw the tears streaming down my face. But then, when I turned around—I thought I saw tears in those seamed and hardened faces looking back at me.

Printed in the United States
By Bookmasters